Mini Pigs

or

Miniature Pigs

A Practical Guide To Keeping Mini Pigs.

by

Steward Stevenson

D1291221

1

Published by: IMB Publishing

Table of Contents

Foreword

Your child cannot resist it but neither can you! If you see it from their end, i.e. from staring live on popular TV shows to seeing them on YouTube, life doesn't seem to be that uninteresting for these cute mini – or micro or teacup – pigs either. It is the new thing in town to have these popular animals around.

To the delight of many, however, that's not all. Unlike the challenges provided for by the other types, mini pigs boast of a couple of exotic personality traits that make them such wonderful pets.

But what's better than impulsive buying? It's about understanding their type and getting acquainted with their needs that allows you to properly care for them and, subsequently, claim yourself as a good piggy parent. This book has been compiled to help you find the information that can help you take care of your miniature pig.

Introduction

A cat looks down upon a man, and a dog looks up to a man, but a pig will look a man in the eye and see his equal.

– Winston Churchill

Let's admit it, we have always been too fond of the creature.

The Rise of the Pocket Pig

It seems appropriate to delve into a little history here, bust some myths, and see what it is about these pigs (besides the fact that they are cuddly) for people like Paris Hilton, Rupert Grint and Victoria Beckham to consider having one in their house. What factors made them replace dogs, cats, small rodents, fish, and birds as faithful companions to Man, so much so that many breeders have a long line of waiting prospects?

It began with Keith Connell. As a Canadian zoo director in late 1985, he imported 20 <u>unrelated</u> Vietnamese potbellies, a breed of domesticated pigs that are significantly smaller and weigh less than the standard farm pigs in USA and Europe.

Where they were initially being developed and used for medical research, the act became a foundation to having them as pets in apartments and homes. That was not the intention of the person himself who saw no purpose for them than their ability to draw visitors' attention at an exhibit in Europe.

The law stated that he was not permitted to sell any from the original stock of 18 – two of them had died either in quarantine or in travel – but that he could export/sell the offspring. The Connell Line, reportedly in black color, is renowned as the most pure Pot-Bellies.

A second name to join his in history is that of Keith Leavitt, who was responsible for the Lea Line in the US. Their ancestors were brought from Europe in 1989. They can be kept as pets in the US but out of those the Pot-Belly's lineage can be traced to an original stock in the USA or Canada.

A third name for some would be that of Chris Murray of Devon, who declared that the micro and "teacup pig" are the same. He is known to be the original breeder of the latter, after unveiling one in Pennywell in 2007. This is despite the fact that breeding for micro pigs began as early as 1992 in the U.K.

When evolution took over, it was hard to keep the backyard/private/counterfeit breeders aloof. Whether it was from underfeeding them or inbreeding the lines, the aim of these individuals was to initiate a lucrative industry that was unregulated for most parts.

In order to keep track of the pedigrees, the Potbellied Pig Registry Service, Inc. (PPRSI) was created; it was dissolved in the late 1990s but not before another, by the name of the Miniature Potbellied Pig Registry Service, Inc. (MPPRSI) had a chance to establish itself in 1993.

Chapter 1) What are they really?

The problem comes when most buyers contacting agencies are cheated into believing that the weight of these animals would remain the same regardless of how old they got. When they grow up, these people naturally are left frustrated. To begin with then, it is important that you consider fancy terms such as micro-minis as a relative term, implying no more than for the creature to be smaller in size when compared to their counterparts in the farm. A true breed of potbellied pig weighs well under 100 lbs., which, when compared to the standard 1000 lbs of a farm hog, would make it a miniature.

A **Potbelly Pig** is characteristically small, short-legged, has tasseled ends on their straight tail, pointed ears, and short to medium nose. The weight range varies as it matures; the back shapes out to be slightly swayed, grows short and stiff bristles as hair, and is often black in color though crossbreeding has given way to different black and white combinations as well as pure white pigs.

Also known as the Vietnamese potbellied pig, its appearance along with its docile temper makes it an instant favorite for apartment owners. On average they can weigh 120-200 pounds and grow up to about 16-26 inches.

A potbelly that is slightly smaller than this regular size is usually categorized as a **Mini Potbelly Pig**. However, this is not for you to believe that there is a lot of difference with respect to the size and weight for them when compared to their counterparts. They will be somewhere around 15-16 inches in height and will easily weigh around 80-120 pounds.

A third category for the same, the **Micro Pig or Micro Potbelly Pig**, is the smallest of them all, which you will be able to buy as a pet. You have to be careful in buying the breed that's sold under this name because many are known to still carry a significant amount of weight with them, averaging at 60-80 pounds with a height between 12-14 inches. These are the pigs that celebrities carry around in their handbag.

What's known as the "teacup pigs' is basically the generation that's been bred off the Gloucester Old spot. But guess what? Theirs is a weight in the range of 40-65 pounds and a height between 12-20 inches. Surprising, right?

Another type is the **Guinea Hog or the African Pigmy Pig** that are thought to have originally come from West Africa to the southern parts of the USA. They are unique and rare. From huge and hairy, these have evolved to be shorter with a straight back, sturdy build, medium sized ears, and a curl to their tail. The snout is moderate, their forequarters slightly shorter than the hind ones, and the nape of the neck shows off a slight thickening and bristling while the skin is generally non-wrinkled.

In character, they have been recorded as highly intelligent, active, and like to be close to the people they get attached to. These can grow to a height of 14-24 inches and weigh 20-40 pounds when they are fully-grown. They are usually black.

A third type is the **Ossabaw Island Pigs** that, regardless of having been crossed with multiple domestic breeds in USA, have kept their original strain that gives them their heavy coats, long snouts, and prick ears. Colors include blue, gray, and red with spots that are both black and white whereas the stripes can have a variety from black, white, calico, and red. As far as their disposition is concerned, they have a very lively nature and are easy to train and bond with. They can, quite literally, be treated as children. Weighing 25-90 pounds, and averaging around 14-20 inches in height, they can live up to 25 years.

The **Juliana Pig** has a European background. More petite and small compared to the potbellied pig, these tend to have longer snouts, straight backs, longer legs, and a spotted back, which attributes their lean and athletic appearance. They are gentle but outgoing creatures, weighing not more than 50 pounds and are 10-15 inches high on the healthy side.

The **Mexican Hairless or Yucatan Pig** has a proud ancestry in Central America and Mexico. They do not have a potbelly, have very thin hair coats, straight backs, short snouts, and ears that are medium-sized. Very gentle, they come in black and slate-gray color, a height of 16-24 inches, and a weight of 50-100 pounds that on the extreme can turn 200 pounds when they mature.

A final breed type, the **Kunekune Pig**, is known for their turned-up, short-sized snout with the more distinctive two tassels (called wattles) that hang from their lower jaw. They are round and short, and make for delightful company, as they are extremely laid-back and friendly. The hair, whether straight or curly, short or long, is in combinations of ginger, brown, black, gold, spotted, and cream. They are about 150-250 pounds heavy and 24 inches high.

To stress the point made earlier, since owners are able to influence only the weight of the pig – its length and height being predetermined by genetics – the phenomenon can be attributed to the fact that their diet and exercise are controlled to maintain their preferred shape, especially during the first two years of their growth.

a) Does this mean that the teacup variety does not exist?
Precisely. What have been sold off so far as a result of frantic attempts are not normal or healthy otherwise. A breed that's this desirable will always be capitalized on.

The order that's claimed is always the same: micros being the smallest of the lot with a weight range of 25-35lbs (anything smaller than 25 will be the super micros); tea cups bag the second position with a weight range of 35-55lbs for 18 months old. The miniatures will be 65-85 lbs while a regular would be over 85lbs. For the same age in terms of their height (measured at the shoulder) micros range from around 10-11", the teacups have 12.5-15", miniatures get to be 15.5-18", and the regulars are more than 18" tall.

It was necessary to clear this misconception in the beginning to ensure that the pig you'll be buying won't be left homeless in a hurry simply because it was unable to satisfy this perception. Seeing as how they all share the breed line, even a "plump" appearance say in a 100 pound pig would add up to size of a small dog weighing only 35-40 pounds.

b) And if you still are still in love with them?
They get along great with other pets, especially cats. Since pigs are hard-wired as herd animals, each tries to be the dominant one among the group, to warn other piglets if there's danger. So, you should not leave them alone for too long or else they are likely to suffer from depression. Apart from that, they are very intelligent, clean and can live up to 10-15 years. However, given the commitment of the owners, some live for as long as 18-20 years.

On the downside, you have to deal with their suspicious approach to everything, their stubbornness, and yes, even manipulation.

What began as a genuine recreational interest by Connell gave way to a complete new trade: miniature pigs. But like all other business, the market has its share of fraud stories. Even so, to say that these creatures don't earn themselves a place in our heart and among our family would be an understatement. In the types of Vietnamese potbellied pig, the Guinea Hog, Ossabaw Island Pigs, the Juliana Pig, Mexican Hairless, and the Kunekune breed variety, they are generally great to have in your apartments and around your family and other pets.

Chapter 2) Things to Consider Before Buying a Miniature Pig

The one question that any purchase boils down to, i.e. if you exhaust yourself with the wants vs. needs debate in your mind before buying something, is whether it's right for you. In terms of miniature pigs, how well you score on a few factors can help you determine if you are actually doing the right thing.

1) Are You Ready for a Mini Pig?
It's one of the most basic and yet skipped over questions to date regarding mini pig adoption. Many people mistakenly, readily too, believe that a pig will be like any other pets. Well, not to burst your bubble but in terms of training, intelligence, and habits, nothing can be more of an understatement than this.

You shouldn't be considering buying them just because you want to have one and would rather have anything than a dog that you don't like.

This is not the time either to carry any misconception regarding the animal. Without a doubt, there will be no 'happily ever after' in your personal story. Pig or pigs, irrespective of their size, can be quite a handful; you have to take care of them, complying in the meantime with rules set by both the state and your landlord, and reassuring yourself or children that there's no need to send this one to an animal shelter in due time.

Therefore, to be on the safe side, it's best to begin with this matter.

2) Do You Know Your Facts?
We read how mini pigs have been a result of selective breeding for a couple of generations. This was done to bring them down to a size that could make them ideal as indoor pets. For that purpose, research the breed to know what you can expect it to look like once it is fully-grown. A hint to let your imagination work for the

13

typical heights mentioned in inches in compatibility with weight in pounds, a matured mini pig would be similar to a small or medium-sized dog.

Most of the breeders often use this one tactic to sell off young piglets as "miniature pigs", i.e. use young pigs only to breed another. And by young I mean pigs as young as four months old, their only problem being that they can breed.

So, if you are smart enough to demand a look at their parents, they will produce these tiny pigs as the legal parents and claim for your little one to grow up just the same! For an unsuspecting buyer, the intro would prove useless as the pig typically grows to its full height on its third birthday, and gains weight until they reach four or five years of age according to their genes.

The piglet(s) you are interested in might have been receiving a 'special' diet. A point to direct you on this front would be if the breeder welcomes you as a potential buyer with a contract to feed your new baby exactly as they recommend, not less and especially not more. Surprisingly, some even go as far as to supply secondary owners with the food items, saying that anything beyond that would constitute a violation of their contract.

The idea behind these limited proportions is obviously to stunt the piglet's growth. Unfortunately insufficient nutrition instigates extremely aggressive behavior and other major health issues. If hey don't get enough to eat, it doesn't take them long to turn aggressive by biting, tearing apart carpets, cupboards, and even jump on you or the dining table in search of any crumbs.

If you are seeking a "pure breed", you might want to check with your breeders again. This is because inbreeding to concentrate desired traits exhibited by a specific type is not considered the ideal practice for any specie. It often leads to many congenital abnormalities and with miniature pigs being no different, these may include reduced immunity, low bone density, and diminished mental capacity just so you can have smaller and smaller sized pigs.

Consider for example the case of a tiny pig that had been given oatmeal and yogurt as per the instructions from the breeder just to end up with major pain in its legs and shoulders.

Practically, the second point to ponder over would be whether you want a creature as <u>intelligent</u> as a pig – FYI, they are listed among the world's smartest animals including apes and dolphins. Don't jump to answer it with an overwhelming "Yes, of course!" as they can be quite sly and cunning.
Most breeders have listed the micros as a perfect indoor pet. This is not to say that they are 100% wrong but it is not the complete truth either.

Categorized as the fourth most intelligent creature, pigs too have complex emotions to deal with. So when you come across a pig in a sanctuary that is displaying negative behavior, it is likely to be the result of being placed in a strange and stressful environment, mourning the families who have abandoned them.

To elaborate on behavioral issues, you should know that it is rare for pigs, even the mini ones, to live inside the whole time. Yes, they love lounging on your soft bed, they love watching TV and being part of your family but they also need to go sniffing and rooting in the dirt outside. It's a prerequisite for something that spends at least 40% of the time doing that in the wild. Not catering to their instinctively curious natures can become an issue for your home in general and furniture in particular. It's innocent despite their ability to remember stuff and how once they get the feel for their environment, they will be running around your place. Plus, for some, it may mean overturned trashcans, torn up flooring, or overturned plants.

Their manipulation is not easy to overcome. Much like us, their intelligence facilitates them in keeping up with an ultimate goal. Keeping food as a primary motivator for such tricks, they will not only identify a weak spot quickly but also remember it and make sure to exploit it for their benefit. If you think that learning a trick is just part of their conditioned behavior to earn their prize, then you are mistaken. They are 'wise' enough to know which of these may prove most advantageous. From learning to open the cabinets/fridge doors to sitting and performing for food, you'll find them on their marks to score.

As far as their reliability goes, they enjoy interaction with people. They crave attention so people who are home a lot would make ideal parents. They can be trusted with small children but it is wiser not to leave both unsupervised. Alternatively, they are preferred for households that have older children.

They haven't posed any problem either where living with other animals is concerned.

Despite the fact that they are usually quiet animals, they scream if they are not given their own way or are frightened. Most of them can also steal food from cupboards and the fridge to fill their endless appetites.

If you think you can handle this, think about the fact that, like humans, pigs are known for their unique personalities. They can be gentle but they are also playful and very social animals. Can you see where this is going? It implies about 12-20 years of loving companionship, which can be fun but not so much if you prefer peace and quiet. Their lifespan varies too according to the strong attachments that they form with people, the treatment they receive, and their dependency on their caretakers.

The advanced mental capacities of these breeds make them socially dependent to a greater degree. In expressions and communication too, they rank high above the standard growling and barking one is usually accustomed to, using both verbal and body language for that purpose. For every time that they anticipate something delightful and desirable or when they want to pass a greeting, you can literally be overwhelmed with their laughter and squealing; if you annoy them or they sense potential danger, this will be replaced with a deep coughing and growling.

They squeal in pain. For contentment, a pig makes pleasant, quiet noises.

The body postures ensue usually from either a challenged, spoiled, or an unhappy pig that wants to maintain their social position. From throwing the head around to wagging their ears or clicking the jaw, the responses can tip you off about your pet's mood at present.

They crave close companionship, which sets them apart from other animals. Apart from the socializing aspect, they need the body heat and closeness that comes with the pack, which means you'd find them cuddling up to you at unexpected times and in bed too.

Besides the need for companionship, as pack animals they will follow a leader. The absence of one will lead them to take up the role as a result of which you may be dealing with a more demanding and aggressive pig than the one you bargained for.

Keeping pigs as pets is like having a 3-year-old child for 20 years. You'll constantly be on your toes. You need to have experience dealing with dogs at least to be able to handle the high levels of activity that come with mini pigs. They prefer an owner who has a good sense of humor and lots and lots of patience.

If you are telling them not to root outside, it'll be like asking them to wait until you leave home. They need the guidance from the "top" pig (i.e. you), one who can keep up with their thinking processes. At your end, it asks for a lot of commitment in both time and energy because they need interaction and activity, entertaining distractions in other words, to ward off restlessness and boredom if they are asked to spend inordinate amounts of time alone.

Remember that they function by intuition, instinct, and memory without any conscience or a sense of what's right or wrong. So you need to stay a step ahead of your pig, or in learning and mastering quickly a few simple tricks they'll have you trained exactly as what suits their fancy! If you have a busy schedule, then you are better off without a miniature pig that needs your attention for as long as 15-20 years in order to remain healthy and fit.

There are a few merits to each sex but it doesn't necessarily make any one better than the next. The choice is made according to your individual preferences.

The spayed female is generally a little more active and demanding whereas the neutered males tend to be easier going and laid back.

Fixing the piggy enables you to have an animal that can bond with you. In more cases than one, these have been known to stay smaller too. Boars are not known for their calm natures; they'll chomp their teeth, mark their territory with a frothy foam (and its foul smell) as well as with a pungent liquid; they have long and thick tusks and would keep off unless they want to hump someone. They are also prone to testicular cancer.

Females become sexually active when they're around 12 weeks old. They will go into their heat cycle every 21 days, each of them lasting for about 5-7 days. Their hormonal change is very strong, making them very restless, moody, territorial, and very vocal. They lash out and jump on anything and anyone to breed. There is also the problem of intact females not caring for or forgetting their potty training, urinating in multiple places to "mark" themselves for the boar. They are also susceptible to critical uterine tumors and mammary cancer.

3) Buying vs. Adopting a Miniature Pig

Opinions vary on this front. Many people would rather have a pocket pig from a shelter home, preferring to save the ones that already need your help, than listing your name for a new one and fueling a never-ending game. Not to say that a pig, in spite of its size or other defects, may have been trained already.

Frankly speaking, it's not meant for everyone, more so if you are suspicious as to why its previous owner let the older pig go. In addition, it won't be an easy task to teach the pig some new tricks. While it may be appealing to some how these homes providing love and care for the abused or neglected ones even give these pets for free, you may be risking your first experience due mainly to the lack of knowledge the other owner had.

A rescue then is best saved for the experienced owners for they will have the patience, time, general knowledge, and extraordinary animal training skills to fix the problem and care for it properly.

a) What makes a trusted breeder?
As it becomes a lucrative money making industry, it becomes harder for a person not to be duped by scheming 'owners'. Where most of the sanctuaries duly blame *all* breeders for the increasing numbers of the min-pigs rescued, they and individual buyers are yet to understand that a reputable breeder knows that they are the ones responsible for the pigs that they bring into the world.

That said, the trusted breeders are not the ones who intentionally breed the runts of every litter with other runts just so they can have smaller micro pigs. In allowing only the healthiest stock to produce piglets, they consider it their duty to neuter and spay the piglets, hand them over to well-informed and dedicated parents, and supposing that something still goes wrong, will work to find them new homes.

They ought to have a site or some sort of social media presence too. By posting updated photos and/or videos of the micro pigs as well as their parents, they imply that there is nothing to hide. They will be consistent in showing up with detailed information on training, behavior, etc. Furthermore, they will be supportive of and encourage visits, usually through an appointment, before you buy a pig from them so that you are familiar with the size, build and other intricacies prior to purchase and so that you do not feel cheated. It will also give you an insight as to whether a pig would make a great pet for your household.

Note: There's a difference between showing up to check the one you liked and seeing *all* the baby pigs first and picking the one that seems to like you. It is likely that a lot of breeders would be avoiding the latter and rightly so! Piglets are not to be treated like kittens and puppies. Besides being slightly claustrophobic, most people term them unfriendly too; most untrained pigs run off and hide the first time they see a stranger.

Pigs bond and interact with those who they are with daily and since early on in life. So it won't be natural for them to be crowding around you and asking you to play with them and pet them when they don't know you.

When buying off of them, a good breeder will make you familiar with what's involved in taking care of these pigs as pets, give you background information, and tell you your legal requirements as transporter, keeper, and owner. They will also be willing to offer you quality advice and assistance after the sales should your or the little one require it. They won't feel tired of your questions.

It's clearly a red flag if the breeder is taking guarantee for the weight of the piglet because there's no way any genuine breeder can do that, knowing particularly that they are not the one in control of its care anymore. Yes, they will give an estimate figure based on what a healthy and nutritious diet can be expected to achieve coupled with how the parents have turned out, verifying too that the pig would eventually weigh MORE than the popularly acclaimed 30 pounds.

Why should you care if your breeder is a good one or not?
As long as you are able to get a piglet at a reasonable price and especially when you've researched the breed you are about to purchase etc, it doesn't makes sense right?

Wrong.

Knowing the type of breeder you obtain the piggy from increases your chance of obtaining a quality one to bring into your family. Chances are it will turn out to be less of a burden than most of the others. It is not only you who should have the respective knowledge but the breeder who has put up these varieties of pigs should have the time to be educated as well to ensure they keep the stock free of hereditary diseases, screening them and scheduling them for proper treatments, raising them, additionally, in a good environment.

Like other points, there have been cases of rescued minis suffering from deep recessed eyes or females born without an anus simply because the authority concerned had poor breeding practices to begin with; some produce a herd of 50-100 teacups from a single pair of siblings.

While other factors like cost, distance, and availability matter too, you should think about the costs you could incur on the long-term basis if the piglet turns out to be an embarrassment or a liability to you. Besides, a little more research would tell you that a breeder who is not doing a good job at raising these will be charging the same as another who has taken the pains and spent a hefty amount of dollars on just one litter because they know that most buyers cannot differentiate one from another. Also, it should caution you rather than appeal that a breeder is willing to work with you concerning payment over time.

Secondly, it is possible that the right piglet (from the right breeder too) lives in a state different from yours. But, if you consider that there are many other ways to get a piglet, especially if the right breeder happens to be an experienced shipper as well, then it may not seem to be such a problem for you.

Third, addressing the availability issues, you have to concede to the fact that piglet buyers are placed on a waiting list just so they can have the right pet from the right breeder.

c) Questions to ask the breeder
Since you want to keep a pig as a pet, you would want what's best for them in life, wouldn't you? For that matter, the only way is to know them better, made possible only if you put forth the right questions to its breeder.

21

How old are the mini pigs when they are fully weaned?

Although mini pigs sold at 4-5 weeks appear "cute", it is best if they are at least 8 weeks old before you take it away from its mother. It depends on the individual litter, some taking longer than others to be considered ready to move away from their parent.

They won't develop a strong bond with you if you buy them young, as many breeders are likely to tell you. You can be satisfied that they had sufficient antibodies and nutrients from their mother in the first 4 weeks of their existence. In addition to being healthy, a piglet that old will also be well socialized after having remained with their siblings and mother for this time and will be less stressed upon making the transition.

Is the piglet de-sexed?

Having pigs as pets necessitates that you have them spayed or neutered. Make sure a specialist has treated them. Although males can be neutered as early as 3 days, not everybody does that; you must ensure therefore that it was done before turning 3 months of age or else they may show some residual boar taints. For females, age is not so much of a concern. Ideally, they should be spayed as early as 6 weeks.

Has the pig been vaccinated?

Additionally, ask them whether the piglet has been checked by a vet before leaving and whether it has been dewormed.

If the breeder is as good as they appear to be, they would make available a veterinarian record for the piglet and would in fact have it seen by a licensed doctor. Since vaccination is crucial to ward off their susceptibility for certain diseases, they will start taking preventive measures since the day the baby pigs are born. Additionally, they will try to avoid human exposure.

Unlike the weight, most conscientious breeders will offer you a health guarantee that varies from some days to a year for their pigs. For them, the health of their pigs is a matter of great pride.

They will even have the piglet wormed at least once prior to sending it off to you.

What sort of an environment has been provided to the pigs?
This is an important question to differentiate the type of treatment your pig has been receiving and to determine the behavior that they'll likewise be revealing later. Giving value to some sanctuaries is that they provide a large, natural space for them to grow compared to how the more traditional facilities keep a huge number of them – or are forced to do so by circumstances such as limited funding, workers, land, time – over a quite small and confined area.

This is in direct relation to what was discussed above, i.e. pigs, regardless of whether they are miniature and not commercial hogs, are fond of exploring and wandering in their environment. The freedom that comes with space allows them to engage in activities – grazing, swimming in a pond, wallowing in the mud holes, or roaming and basking in the sun satisfactorily. It also provides them with much needed exercise that improves more specifically the health of their muscles and joints, of their cardiovascular system, wearing down their hoods and burning the extra calories. That is why the parent pigs are kept in a clean environment, are provided with some natural light and an outdoor area in general and adequate shade (during the summer days) and shelter (during the cold) in particular.

A reputable sanctuary would check each pig at least once every day, while the pig patrols go about ensuring that the perimeter remains secure and that the barns and run-in sheds are intact without necessarily interrupting their routine. However, since interaction is a special part of the training pigs have in their earlier days, someone is always around to interact at their comfort level and convenience. There's no forcing any one of them. The time spent interacting with these pigs should make the breeder able to educate you about each parent pig's personality type. The better socialized a parent pig is, the same you can expect in their piglets.

Special needs: Not unlike other animals, pigs have their own sets of needs and wants that have to be given a priority by someone who is supposedly fostering them. The feeding should only be supplementing what they are primarily scouring from the natural environment with an exception made for the winter season to keep each of them at their optimum weight.

The miniature pigs have been shown to mingle in social groups that can have members as low as four to five and as many as twenty pigs. Herds rarely break up and each is lead by a matriarch setup.

Is there a return/exchange policy?
Yes, there is a return/exchange policy on buying live animals. Most pet stores have a return within 14 days policy, and if you change your mind about keeping the pet, return it within this time.

However, sadly, some pet stores do not refund the pet once sold. Therefore, before you choose the place to shop for your miniature pig, check their terms and conditions. Often, there is an upside to having a strict return or purchase policy.

Because these pets are very emotional in nature, they tend to develop emotional attachments. It might happen that despite your efforts to make it happy and comfortable, it just can't settle in and you have to take it back. Make sure that if you feel that returning your pig because it is missing its companions is better to keep it alive; the pet store should take it back.

However, there is more to the return and exchange policy. Some people take the pet home but fail to take good care of it. After the ending date of the return policy, they take the pet back to get rid of additional costs that medical attention would incur. When this happens, pet stores refuse taking the pet back because the buyer is responsible for the condition of the pet.

This might seem wrong to many, but when you look at it from the pet stores' perspective, they are already taking care of several homeless animals and they need customers who they can trust to take good care of the pets. When people don't take care of the pet, they take things seriously because they are dealing with the lives of real animals.

This is also why some pet stores have a strict policy that once you buy the pet, they will bear no responsibility as soon as the handover is complete. These pet stores take extraordinary care of their pets and they take things very seriously with pet buyers. They expect the same caring and proper handling by people.

When it comes to exchanging, although some pet stores are open to the option, others are not. Their reasons vary, but before you consider exchanging the pet, make sure your decision is justified. Why did you choose this particular pet in the first place? If you exchange it, what do you want in return?

It is reasonable if the gender of the miniature pig became the reason for you to change your mind. Perhaps you felt this particular one was too noisy or the fur became a problem; then how sure are you that the next one would be quieter? Whatever the reason is, make sure it is a genuine one and you won't have more reasons to exchange the next one too. It will be better for you to try to understand the pet you adopted rather than returning it, because it does need a home and it will get used to you within fourteen days.

The purpose of imposing limitations on return and exchange policies is that when people adopt pets, they need to take it seriously and treat them well. Pet stores try to look out for the wellbeing of pets that leave their facility.

4) Checklist

✓	Visit prior to buying/adoption	The piglets are so small, they can easily fit in the palm of your hand. Take out time to spend some time around them. Besides, you'll be able to take a good look at its parents along with the other stock a breeder has. It is recommended that you buy registered mini pigs with a pedigree.
✓	The environment	Making a commitment to owning this kind requires you to have a large, fenced off area at hand to keep them. Needless to say, an apartment wouldn't be good for them. An average residential garden doesn't suit them either; the more space they have, the better. Build them a shelter to keep them out of the cold and heat and you can have them outside the whole time. A stable with a bed of straw in a corner can do the job. The materials for building pens – galvanized boards, wood, etc. – do not matter if you can keep the sleeping area draft-free and dry. However, you have to be careful about the fencing. This is because once it has successfully got its nose through, it will try to the best of its ability to wiggle the rest of its body out as well. A wooden enclosure can work but it works best with electrical wires.
✓	The diet	They need a diet that is 16% (or less) protein and more fiber than commercial pigs. If you cannot afford a bigger area for them, they'll still be content with a diet that

		includes fruits and vegetables, hay, or low-protein pot bellied pig pellets and grass pellets. Supplement for the grass and vegetables of summer with apples in autumn; in winter give it approximately 1 lb. grass pellets and water mixed with a 1 lb. weaner and 16% protein sow meal in a hot mash. However, if you are supplying a diet purely based on pig pellets, then the estimated quantities are 0.5kg, 0.75kg, and 1-1.5 kg for a pig that's respectively 2-4 months old, 4-9 months old, and an adult. But then these are not hard and fast rules. If you believe your pig is getting too fat, common sense can direct you to feed it less. The quantities can be lowered too if you are giving them other feed. Of course, quality and ample grass are important components to ensure they are not malnourished when they are at their growing stage.
✓	The number	They are highly social animals and if there aren't any for the purpose, it is likely to become lonely and suffer. Therefore, buy two if you can.

What to avoid: Pet pigs are special animals. You cannot just feed them scraps of waste food, which by definition includes eggs or eggshells, meat/offal or other parts of a livestock/poultry carcass, kitchen or table refuse and anything else too that has contact with it.

5) Where to Buy Them in USA and UK

It is important to select the right place to buy your miniature pig.

Important: Please note I have not bought pigs from any of the websites mentioned in this book. There are many breeders trading on the web purely for money, without thinking about the well being of the pig enough. Please make sure you check out breeders thoroughly before you buy from them.

a) In the U.S
If you are in the U.S. then here are some recommendable websites to check out:

VeetStreet.com: This is an online store where you can get your pet and other items that you will need to raise it. You can also find some amazing tips and guidelines on how to keep your pet healthy and train it well. You need to subscribe to access the store and to enjoy the benefits of being a part of this website.

WhenPigsFlyNaked.com: This website is one of the best places to order your pig, and they make sure they deliver it to you when and wherever you want. In fact, if you need help with guidance on how to potty train it, bath timings, feeding it, understanding it and anything related to your pet, this is the website you need to visit.

LittlePigFarm.com: This is also a highly recommendable online pig shop for people in the U.S. You can read all about miniature pigs and check the charts to know what food quantity is ideal for your pet according to its body weight. They've simplified things a lot. If you plan to farm pigs, there is a lot of information here on that too.

TeaCupPigsForSale.org: This website is one of the largest pig suppliers in the U.S. and they make sure that their pets are in good health and of excellent breed. If you truly love piglets, you will want to place an order right now after visiting this site.

PennyWellPigs.com: For pig pet lovers, this website can be a gold mine of information. You will find everything you need to know right here. You can check their store and shop for the piglet you want to own. You can even go through their gallery and checkout other useful links related to breeding and raising pigs.

b) In the UK

If you are in the UK, then here are some recommendable websites to check out:

Preloved.co.uk: This is an online store for second hand stuff, but people also use it as a platform to sell miniature pigs. You might be lucky to find your pet piggy here and bring it home, so make sure you check it out.

PetPiggies.co.uk: This website remains dedicated to encouraging people to adopt piglets and give them a home. If you are one of those people who are willing to share their love with pigs, then this is where you will find your pet for sure. If you need guidance with raising it and caring for it, then there is a lot of helpful information that you can get here.

LancashireMicroPigs.co.uk: Yes, this website is in Lancashire but it is not limited to piggy owners in Lancashire. If you want to buy your pet piggy from anywhere in the UK, then this is where you will find a huge variety of micro pigs and teacup pigs, all of which are miniature pigs. They have information regarding pig health, toys they love, and a special FAQ page dedicated to questions new pig owners usually ask. Check it out!

MicroPigshed.com: To make the entire experience of adopting and raising your pig even more special, this website has an eBook dedicated to everything you need to know about miniature pigs. You can also find some interesting videos in their video gallery; get training tips and lots more.

PennyWellPigs.com: This website is not just for people in the US but is also accessible to people in the UK. Owners of pigs in the UK will also find the information here very useful and placing an order online is a very smooth process. There is no hassle and you will get your pet piggy within no time; just check out their sales page.

ValleyOfThePigs.co.uk: The owner of this website is the founder/breeder of the British Micro Pig, and has been providing pigs to people since 1996. Here, you will find the most rare and amazing miniature pigs, coming from the heart of the valley of the pigs. Go through their gallery, choose the piglet you love and place an order. It is as simple as that!

NewsNow.co.uk: This is also one of the largest online stores, where people sell not only pigs, but other animals as well. You can shop for miniature pigs here, but make sure the breeder provides proper certification of health and registration.

Friday-ad.co.uk: This is also another online market, where you can find miniature pigs on sale at amazing prices. Like all other online animal markets, you need to be sure that the miniature pig you choose has a proper health certificate and registration. Make sure the breeder can handle delivery and transportation.

Chapter 3) Taking Care Of Your Miniature Pigs

Pigs have been domesticated for a couple of thousand of years and yet it was only some years ago that the exotic animal was considered as a household pet by people like you who realized and approved of their uniqueness. We know they are intelligent, sensitive creatures. They are curious, mischievous and food-crazy with the latter being the cause of many of their attempts at being manipulative. They aren't like any other pets you might have come across. It takes special people to not misunderstand their "pig-headedness" or expect them to blatantly forget their foraging nature. They need to be allowed to be, well, pigs.

A training program tailored to suit their personalities will give you every opportunity to be exhilarated seeing how positive reinforcement from your side turned your shy baby into a loving companion. And that won't be coming from their 'motivation' to please you as its owner. Oh no, they can do better, they deserve better in fact, than that. The simulation therefore is something that would keep them occupied. So, basically, you pamper and train them, but more importantly you respect them knowing that is the only way they'll like you in return and follow your lead with respect to the family social order.

1) What's It Going to Take?
You are essentially adding another member to your family. It's a big decision. Now that you've found THE ONE, you've got other regulations to check up on.

a) Pre-purchase preparations

Check the zoning rules
Pigs are categorized as livestock animals. Before you go ahead with the adoption procedure, check whether the law in your area permits you to have one. Zoning rules are different for each

municipality, town, city, and state. What you should do to confirm the legality of owning a potbelly in the town or city you are in or plan to move to is to contact the zoning department of that municipality.

Most of them usually have it lumped with the livestock laws and would comment, upon inquiry, that these are meant for the breeder and feeder of the pigs. Or they would refer to the laws that were made before the pots even came to the country. The bottom line is that if they are giving you a go-ahead, get it in writing.

According to one resource, the cities that have passed the zoning ordinance for these pets include

- Phoenix, Goodyear, Case Grande, Bullhead City, Yuma, Scottsdale, Apace Junction, Payson – Arizona
- Los Angeles County, San Francisco (county & city), Vacaville, Riverbank, West Hollywood, La Mesa, Palo Alto, Beverly Hills etc. – California
- Denver, Federal Heights, Aurora, Lakewood, Northglenn, Arvada, Eaglewood etc. – Colorado
- St. Petersburg, Ft. Meyers, Safety Harbor, Dade City, Pinellas Park, Lee County, Pascoe County – Florida
- Maroa, Chicago – Illinois
- Plymouth, Austin – Indiana
- Waukesha – Wisconsin
- Kansas City, Hutchinson, Nickerson, Wichita – Kansas
- Lincoln Park, Wayland – Michigan
- St. Louis, Kansas City – Missouri
- Omaha, Hawthorne – Nebraska
- Lynn – Massachusetts
- Chattanooga – Tennessee
- Zimmerman – Minnesota
- Billings, Miles City – Montana
- Reno - Nevada
- Vancouver, Prosser, King County, Palouse, Seattle – Washington

- Gloucester County, Camden County – New Jersey
- Akron, Cincinnati – Ohio
- New York City – New York
- Gresham, Portland, Aumsville, Springfield – Oregon
- Salt Lake City, Provo – Utah
- Hanover County, Chesapeake, Fairfax, Henrico County, King George County, Roanoke County – Virginia
- Camden County – New Jersey
- Weaverville – North Carolina
- Harrisburg, Wrightsville – Pennsylvania
- Austin, Dallas, Southlake, Kirby, Belton, Grand Prairie, Krum, Fort Worth etc. – Texas

Secondly, make sure to run it past your homeowner's association (HOA) as well if you are part of it to ensure that you can indeed bring the miniature pig into your home.

Other restrictions: The National Animal Identification System (NAIS) provides the 15-digit ID, using a number of tagging methods such as retinal scans and micro-chips to control animals and premises that come in contact with a foreign animal disease within 48 hours of its discovery.

For UK: In order to move a pig onto your premise, you need to have a CPH number. There are no special requirements for you to get one from the Rural Payments Agency (RPA); it doesn't necessitate a home inspection even. The aim is simply keep a trace on the movement of the particular livestock throughout the country so as to help prevent the spread of the disease.

Prepare your home
Before you have it shipped over or ride with one yourself, make sure you have the essentials ready at home to make breaking it in as easy as possible.

Home: To begin with, your pigs need a place to call its own. It's not so much a problem with individuals as it is with a pair of pigs who are not willing to share. Then you are a better judge of their personality.

In options, you have large doghouses, with a size that's 4 x 4"
minimum. Add a porch to their place to serve for it when the
house gets too hot. What's more, measure the door to hang over a
heavy drape in order to block a cold draft. During the summer,
you can roll it up and clip it in place. However, these may not
suffice if your area experiences snowfall.

Next, there is a stockade fence to attend to them sufficiently in a
mild climatic region, i.e. it can protect the pig from rain as well as
have a gentle breeze to keep the baby cool. Just like with the
doghouses, you can provide a narrow deck for this too so the
potbellies can lounge in the sun. If you are planning to keep two
or more in a group, one suggestion is to create multiple exit points
so they can move out if there is a squabble. Keep it over
landscape timbers that have been pressure treated in addition to
building it with a pressure treated floor.

During winters, most people move their pigs into the barn. The
pens to accommodate them must be raised above the floor and
given a wooden bottom to avoid concrete. If needed, you can opt
for a 75-watt or 100-watt light bulb as a brooder lamp with a hood
on the top of each box to keep the pig warm for times they aren't
using their blankets. [On the rare chance that your pig falls sick,
weak, or cold, an infrared lamp is to be used instead. Keep the
lamp raised above a hole on top of the pig's stall with a wire grid
and keep it fastened to so that there is ventilation and there's no
way your pig can reach it.]

Caution: Using heat lamps oblige you to practice extreme
caution. To prevent a fire, you must see that there are no
combustible items nearby and that there is no chance of it being
knocked down. Make sure too that your pig isn't going to succeed
at pushing the bedding close to the lamp. Second, check the
temperature with your bare hand to see if it is bearable.

Give them a deep bed of hay to nestle in, effectively above their
backs, and use blankets to keep them comfortable.

Another thing is that you don't want to cause problems for your neighbors or risk the safety of your pigs. Build them a securely fenced area outside. When planning, you can keep in mind the approximate size your pig is growing up to be.

They can be wood placed as railings across the area. Others have made it with cattle panel only, or done it a split rail style using cattle or hog panels; some loop it (internally) with orange electric fencing tape charged with a low power. The verdict stands thus: the cattle panels are the most secure while the hog and chain link fencing – although at the different low and high ends of the price range – can be climbed over or broken through respectively by a pig determined to escape.

Each of them wants to root instinctively. They cannot help it. But you can. Mark out a spot for him/her where it doesn't matter to you if (s)he roots, especially following rain or in the spring when the ground is soft. Do this instead of curbing their behavior with a nose ring – that's cruel! – or trying to satisfy their need with a rooting box full of plastic balls, round stones or other treats. And don't complain if manipulating it this way to keep it indoors costs you your carpet, bedding, flooring, etc.

If you don't have natural shade at your place to provide for your potbelly, then invest in one that looks promising to you in offering maximum shade. Sweating doesn't help them cool off. It's critical therefore that you take this factor into account when arranging for where the pig's pen is going to be. Buy them either online or contact a farm store whether you are seeking a size to fit a kennel or a greenhouse.

The size is one feature to judge them on. They differ in their levels of protection too. You can take in fancy ones for personalization's sake but a simple lean-to one can be effectively useful and its slanted roof will shield your pig in the rain and simultaneously be able to give it shade from the scorching sun as well.

Water: Your pig is going to be pleasantly surprised if instead of giving it a muddy area to laze around in, you can provide it with a source of fresh water. They use it as both a source to cool off at and to sip from.

It may turn out to be challenging but generally a cubic or triangular pressure treated box measuring 2 x 4" will work well to accommodate an individual. On the other hand, you can give them a child's pool, particularly during the summers. While some do appreciate the gesture by coming to enjoy a splash now and then, even in mid winters, others (from the potbellied type) may stand steadfastly against it.

For a neat animal, they have a tendency to urinate and/or defecate in their pools only. You might have to clean them more than once a day.

Food: Possibly the next appropriate thing to touch upon and discuss would be food for your voracious, omnivorous kiddos. It's precious to them and can be used as the sole motivator to drive them.

The fact that they can eat everything from berries, roots and vegetation, to fruit, meat, grubs, etc is not to imply that you can just give them anything to devour. You cannot give them meat. Furthermore, you cannot give them anything that has a high content of salt either (for instance pretzels) that may result in salt poisoning. A piece or two as a treat is okay but let them get into a bag and you might as well kill it.

A mini pig diet can turn out costly for you at least in the early years when the baby is young and growing. But it's the solution to keep them healthy. A premium among these is the pelleted feed called Mazuri. For the tiny ones, ¼ of a cup thrice a day can do; as they grow, the intake can be increased appropriately, so much that even the largest adult can be given about one to two cups each for mealtimes on a given day. You can try and ensure proper nutrients for them by adding oatmeal and/or baby cereal to it.

Other substitutes can be the Calf Manna pellets or the Milk Plus pellets besides having access to a reliable source of grass and alfalfa mix hay as well as timothy. Fruits and vegetables remain limited.

Arrange for a vet

Yes, the breeder confirmed that they are going to have it checked before the pig exchanged hands, yet you need to find a good, qualified and experienced veterinarian to treat your pigs in both emergencies and to provide regular checkups.

If you have bought a breed that isn't castrated, you need the vet to do this as well because the consequences otherwise as mentioned above won't let it qualify as a 'delightful' pet.

It can prove dangerous to rely on 'help' from the public forums or friends who have never had one nor can you afford to search for a vet at the time that your pet requires medical attention. Just make sure your pet pig undergoes routine vaccinations, routine health checks, dietary advice, tusk trims, hoof trims, and parasite control.

Furthermore, having checked in with one prior to owning the pig can allow you to prepare a first aid kit for your pig for some quick treatments. These can range from the very basic diary and pen to record a symptom, a digital thermometer, and cotton swabs, to the more general oral syringes, sunscreen, a pill crusher, small plastic cup to mix meds, and broad-spectrum antibiotics. Any other ointment or anti-inflammatory steroids or an equipment to add to your inventory in case you needed to diagnose and treat pigs out of necessity for timing or expense (rather than wait and delay) can be discussed with the vet. As a good measure, make sure you check the expiry dates of the medications and replace when needed. No one's asking you to give your pig an injection if you are not comfortable with it, especially given that the latter isn't going to cooperate with you, but this is an important step to determine if you are ready to take the responsibility.

b) Bringing the pet home

Note that in the first place, it is illegal to transport pigs for business purposes without a proper certificate.

It is necessary to look into the policies your state may have regarding the transportation of pigs. Suppose you purchased your miniature pig online, or abroad; and now it is time to get it home, there will be the need for a formal registration and you will also need to acquire the general license for the movement of pigs. The breeder will also need a health certificate before it can come into the state. Usually the cost of the certificate is inclusive in the shipping charges.

Every state has a unique set of requirements, so you need to check with the local authorities. Usually the health certificate must date within ten days of the day it crosses across states.

The age of the piglet also matters. If it is above four months, it will require blood tests and stool screens to screen it for diseases that it can carry. Only a USDA vet can endorse a health certificate, and the state keeps a log of all the certificates. They also inspect the skin, teeth, genitals, ears and rectum of the pigs.

This process is important because it helps owners ensure that the pig is free of health issues, internal and external parasites and has no heart problems as well. However, there are several other health problems that these screening processes may not detect, so getting it checked with your local vet later will still be a recommendation.

The entire screening process may take a week, so you will have to time the arrival accordingly.

Airlines also require an original copy of the certificate, so make sure your breeder emails the copy to you. Make sure that you provide the certificate at every step of the way to ensure the smooth transportation of your new pet.

Crucial information that the health certificate possesses is the vet's contact details. If in future you need to make references to the vet's certification, this comes in handy.

If you are not sure of the requirements of your state regarding the transportation of pigs, then make sure you read about the regulations of your state before making the purchase.

If the breeder is in your state, then you may not need certifications, but only a simple registration to keep a log of the pig in your custody. However, it is always recommendable to get a certification.

When will the piglet be ready for shipping?
The right age for the shipment and delivery of piglets is when they are six to eight weeks old. This should be about the time when they wean off. It is not advisable to purchase and transport the younger ones or the ones that are still breastfeeding because they are frail and delicate. They should be capable of eating on their own before transportation is possible. Although you might be too excited and anxious for the new family member to arrive, waiting a little longer to make sure it is healthy is the best thing to do.

It is also important to mention here that the shipping date and flight availability for the baby pig (piglet) is subject to the climate. You would not want to get it home in harsh weather.

What's the best form of transportation?
The first thing to consider is the distance. If you've purchased the miniature pig from a long distance retailer, then transportation by flight is the best option. This will be less stressful for your piglet because it will arrive home within a matter of a few hours. This usually costs approximately $350 (including health certificate, state permit, and airline approved crate and travel expenses).

Important: It is always best to pick up your piggy, even if you have to rent a special car to do so. I am not in favor of ever shipping animals because of the distress it can cause.

Picking your piggy
For new owners this can be a very sensitive and emotional moment. You will be notified ahead of time regarding the date,

time and place of the pickup so that you are there when your baby arrives.

Ground transportation
If you opt for ground transportation, and if for any reason you cannot get to the pickup place, you can always ask for home delivery. This will cost much less (approximately $200 – inclusive a health certificate, state permit, and airline approved crate and travel expenses).

Do you need pre-notification?
Yes, you need pre-notification before you move any pig from their holdings. You can do this in a number of ways:

Online via Electronic License: You can use this method to report a pig movement and inform the appropriate authority of your state or country.

Fill in the Form: You might have to follow the traditional method of submitting paper work to report the move.

No matter what, before you can move or transport a pig, you must comply with the conditions and requirements of the General License for the Movement of Pigs in your state.

Once you receive your baby piggy, you will have to give it all the love and attention it needs, so the main thing you have to focus on is bonding with it.

c) Bonding with your miniature pig
Pigs not only need attention but also need to be showered with affection for the many years that you are going to have them around. A pig that has companions will trouble you less during your everyday routine. However, if you are not able to provide that, do your part at least in taking the time to give a stimulating environment instead of keeping them in a secluded place.

What's in a name?
You are getting a pig. Maybe it's meant as a gift for your lovely teenager or maybe it's just for you! The news, therefore, should

be exciting for you and even though you do not yet know its personality, it is no excuse for you to be a spoilsport in finding a cute or sophisticated name for your little one. At least you have the gender to fall back on.

We understand your need to think up a unique name for it so consider the following list assembled as a guide to what is termed acceptable in the world of mini pig owners around the world; although what can be better than for you to fall in love with one and adopt it for your own?

Abigail	Alice	Alex	Amber	Amanda
Arnold	Apollo	Audra	Aylott	Bailey
Bentley	Betty	Big Mumma	Blossom	Brian
Buttercup	Casey	Cate	Charlie	Clarice
Cledus	Cleopatra	Cotton	Daisy	Darcy
Dave	Denley	Dolly	Dustin	Eliot
Evelyn	Elleen	Farran	Franky	Garrison
Granny	Griffen	Groucho	Gucci	Hamilton
Hamlet	Hannah	Helga	Heracles	Hermione
Izzy	Janice	James	Jane	Jeremy
Jessy	Jimmy	Jules	Karl	Kevin
Kosher	Leroy	Leslie	Lily	Linda
Lucy	Maggie	Magnum	Marie	Marshal
Martin	Melvin	Miley	Morgan	Muffin
Nathan	Nellie	Nestor	Nicole	Norris
Olive	Ornie	Pabio	Penelope	Petunia
Phineas	Piggy	Phillip	Pink	Pippin
Priscilla	Reese	Rollan	Rose	Sam
Scarlet	Scout	Squishy	Stewart	Sue
Sydney	Talia	Tammy	Toby	Tory
Ulrich	Veronica	Victoria	Wade	Warren
Wiggles	Wilbur	Wombo	Yetta	Zoe

2) House breaking

The instincts of your mini pig can guide you in multiple ways on this front if you let them even as you maintain your authoritative role.

First, prepare a "home" for the pig. The place is to be a confined space meant for you to control them so choose well, whether it is the large bathroom, kitchen, or the laundry room, where you are okay with its bed with a sheet or blanket, its litter box, toys, and the two large, heavy bowls. Some pigs come with a blanket (they love burrowing under them!) and a crate but even then, it is better to have your own supply of medium sized dog or pig pillows. The piglet is to know it is his/hers to stay in so that he/she may not roam freely in a dangerous environment when you are not there to watch out for it.

The provisions for food and litter boxes signify this. It is also important for you to understand the fact that they rely on their trail to the bathroom so you should not move their litter box unless you are able to teach them the way back while increasing their living area. At this time you can potty train him/her with commands like "go potty", not forgetting to praise if he/she is able to use the box properly.

As highly sensitive creatures, pigs interpret a pat on their neck and head from above as a predator move so you may want to consider sitting on the floor beside them and being patient as they warm up to you. You may of course tempt them with food onto your lap(s), petting from their side and working up their body, until they are able to feel safe and comfortable without it as well. Similarly, make sure that you are in a sitting position and reaching from below and not above the head when you are picking the pig for the first time. While taking time out for this would obviously be more generous at your end, you can do the same whenever you are watching TV or chatting at the day's end with your spouse or children. Not only do they enjoy the warmth and comfort when covered with a blanket in your lap, the persistence and frequency enables a greater bonding in addition to developing your position.

Some are frightened and timid, taking weeks to get used to their new place, so a squeal or a scream even is a possibility that you should expecting whenever you try to pick it up. Very much like our own newborn though, you can soothe them by cradling them, holding them tight against yourself in an upright position all the time. Never hold them upside down or your pig is going to take longer than usual to establish the trust. You can even talk to them. Initiate conversation so that your baby piglet learns it and is likewise vocal with you too. You can literally tell that they are excited with the way they begin moving their tails back and forth upon hearing your voice. It will also assist you when teaching them simple commands because they are so accustomed to your voice and particular words such as kiss, twirl, sit, and lay.

The second important aspect for the pig during its first few days will be when you allow him to go outside on special occasions since they are not yet fully reliable. This is because as much as they would rather be roaming outside, keeping them close in the house helps with their bonding.

It is important that you do not mix playtime with potty training when you do take them out. It is possible too that despite your personal attention, the baby has more than one accident in the house. You can either pick him/her up and carry it back or tell him/her "no" to stop while you scoot it back to the box. You cannot blame the small bladder at the time but since the training is crucial for the time he/she grows, you can use any animal odor-neutralizing agent to cover the smell. However, they are really easy to potty train and you will see them preferring to go outside to do it within a few weeks or a month of it. The best part about house breaking is that you don't need to intimidate or bully them into anything; a little love and security is all the pig is looking for on your part to climb and fall asleep in the arms of his new family.

3) Leash training

You have to begin with leash training for your pig, which is if you want to take them in public or on walks, as soon as you feel that he is feeling secure within the new environment. It's natural for them to follow you everywhere since you obviously have spent a lot of time together in getting it acquainted to the new place. You can even teach it to wear a harness. Purchase a pig harness for this purpose, one that you can adjust; it is important to keep within the laws when taking it outside of the home

One way to slip it on him/her is when the mini pig is the happiest. It could be the moment when it is occupied with eating. Don't hurry it into it though. Begin by merely placing it next to its food bowl so that it gets used to seeing it and takes time to ensure that it's not threatening in any way. He/she may walk over it, sniff it, taste it and you can even pick it up and put it down while it is eating so that he/she realizes that you are familiar with it and have in fact placed it there. Your duty is to stay with your pet as it eats, talking and caressing it the whole time. Now that it is satisfied, you can fasten the stomach strap while using a phrase that you want to associate with the process of putting on the harness. Speak softly, move slowly, and adjust the harness so that it is not too tight. Under no circumstances are you to reach down and grab the harness; like a parent to a small child, you need to inform your pig first about what you are doing.

Keep it on for a couple of hours every day, letting it run around with it in the familiar environment to eliminate stress.

If you've reached the stage where the pig wears the harness with minimal protests, you can safely proceed to attach a lead to the harness. You both will have to be in a room with smaller dimensions to it so that the maximum it can go with the lead on is right up against the opposite wall.

Expect them to freak out and turn wild at the start. That's their normal reaction if they feel restrained as prey, so ensure that the leash and harness together with you guiding them is a safe thing.

You are again allowed to use food as bait. Tug on their lead at least twice gently along with a verbal instruction asking them to come forward and eat the food out of your hand. Continue to back up and repeat the whole thing, the only difference being in the decreased amount of food, to make a habit out of it. In removing and replacing the harness as well as walking to a lead, you may train him/her for 15 minutes straight but not more than that, especially if the pig is going all flip-and-spin style.

Always give it a treat before you put the lead on and before you take it out for a walk; try it inside your home, around the garden preferably, with the lead on for 15 minutes approximately. You can keep the lead on whenever the mini pig is in the mood to follow you around the house or outside. Remember, though, that you cannot leave him/her with the harness unsupervised for longer. Remember that it's not going to be easy even with the leash. It understands that it is free as long as it maintains a respectable boundary and it exploits it as much as possible. It can try to control where you both walk and prefer a leisurely stroll to a brisk walk or try to pick up treats along the way. In other words, it's going to try and lead you.

To train it effectively, you have be gentle and compassionate and to continue using the treats rather than forcing it and jerking with the lead. Likewise, it is important that the pig come to take you for a leader so using a phrase like "walk", can make the move in the direction you want to go. Giving it a treat as soon as it gets close to you than staying as far apart as the leash would allow can help you dominate.

4) Grooming

Of course, your pig like any other pet should be given decent grooming. For DIY-owners, the task is made easy knowing that you can use a tail & mane shampoo or a flex conditioner & shampoo.
Bathe the mini pig(s) only when they are smelly or dirty because of the sensitivity of their skin. You can do it once every two months approximately. Hold them close after a bath, caressing,

45

and showering them with kisses. You can also put Cheerios in the tub for them while giving them a bath to get them to relax. You'd need to hold them in a sitting position the whole time and make them feel secure so that they don't start to jump around. You may not need to do this once your pig gets used to having a bath.

Secondly, include a moisturizer rather than applying oil for dry skin. Third, clean its ears of ear mites and wax with a cotton ball and not a Q-tip. And fourth, persuade him/her to rest in your lap as you file its hooves once every month.

Skin Care: It is important that you put a quality baby sunscreen on them if it is going to be out for long periods in the sun.

Hoof Care: You'd be surprised to note just how exactly these mini pigs resemble us. Their hooves are an excellent example. They grow and need to be trimmed in time. If you do not take time out for this, they can make it difficult for the pig to walk, putting a strain on the ligaments and weighing down on multiple pressure points. On the other hand, if you are able to keep up to the task, then you won't need to cut or trim the hooves.

You can do this with a toenail file when they are enjoying a belly rub or cuddle time. It would take only a few weeks' time to become a routine for them.

5) Feeding

You might want to distribute your time and commitment equally in providing these pets the love, shelter, education, and food that they require right away.

They may not require much food in the beginning although of course much depends on how their metabolism works combined with their activity levels. You might want to feed it less if your pig has a slow metabolism and is less active too. The more active he gets or the faster their metabolism gets to be, the more you can feed him on a daily basis. Not to say that the food intake would obviously increase as they mature.

Remember, pigs can eat all day and, as you'll find out with the time spent together, they can easily open cabinets and fridge doors if they have reason to believe you've kept food in there. They may be grazing a good deal too and still tricking you with the "I am starving" act because they don't have a thalamus for their brain to convey to them that they are full. You don't want to end up overfeeding them.

It would be difficult for you to imitate the diet intake they would have enjoyed naturally as omnivores, but you can still establish a healthy routine for them.

Give a piglet a quarter of a cup of pig chow in the morning as well as the evening. Give them a few, small pieces of vegetables and fruits as soon as they can nibble on them and especially as you utilize the time to train them.

Some breeders are known to provide a bag of Mazuri Youth Miniature Pig food that can last for at least three days that they believe have the right amount of protein and fat content to feed the mini pigs. Taking it from there, if you are unable to find a similar pellet feed at your local pet or feed store, you can ask your vet if they would order on your behalf. Popular ones include Manna Pro, Peak Performance, Nutrina, Heartland, and Mazuri by Purina. Some brands, namely Mazuri, have separate feeds categorized as Youth and Active Adult to make it easier for owners to scale up/down the commercial half supplementing their pig's diet.

Other types like the Heartland Feeds do not come with specific feeding guidelines on respective bags. Therefore, while the metabolic rate and activity is what you have to consider, you can give him the Mini-Creep Feed prior to six weeks; the Mini-Starter for piglets that are 6-12 weeks old; the Mini-Grower Feed to be given to pigs from 12 weeks to 5-6 months. The Mini-Pet Feed can serve as the maintenance diet while the Senior Pet Pig Feed can be fed to elder pigs, i.e. those that are over 5-6 years old. You can add Elder-Aide or Elder-Aide GM as well.

Do not soak your piggy's food. Moistening it to a small extent would do the job, that is in case you see your pig making frequent trips to and from the water and food bowls.

You should skip chocolate, avocado, salted popcorn or potato chips because these items have proven to be toxic to pigs. Another thing to be careful about is that fruits should be provided in moderate amounts. Then there is the cat or dog food that pig owners need to be especially be warned about. They lack essential nutrients for a pig and have quite high protein levels for pigs to absorb. There is a reason that cat food is thus named: it's made for cats. Dog food is to be used only in an emergency and for a short time only.

You should also avoid giving them "people food", i.e. the processed foods that are inappropriate for their diet. It is dangerous and cruel to feed it to them because it tends to make them fat and can expose them to other health risks.

Other things that you can feed but only to some extent include spinach (high sodium) fruits (calorie-high) potatoes, sweet potatoes, yams (calorie-high and starchy), corn (sugar-high), and tomatoes (high-acid).

Treats include plain, un-salted air popped popcorn, raisins, shredded wheat, raw seeds or nuts, Cheerios, grapes, and small bits of cheese.

Secondly, they must be provided with clean water. You can install commercial drinkers to let them have access to water on demand. They can be easily obtained from suppliers of pig products and are easy to use as well because the pig just needs to press the tap with its mouth. An alternative to this can be a large concrete bowl or (metal or plastic) containers fixed to the ground.

If you give it fruit juice it will get addicted. It is fine if you can give them this but just to be on the safe side, balance it well by keeping it 100% juice and sugar-free content, increasing the quantity of water in the mixture. But then the best thing for them at any given time is pure water so keep a bowl around. They will drink more in winter or when it's extraordinarily hot.

Pros of Homemade Feed: You may be interested in feeding them a homemade diet. For one, you would know what it is made up of exactly. Reading off a bag's label won't inform you whether the oats included are indeed moldy or fresh.

Some owners also claim that a poorly chosen diet would lead to a stinking pig. They also count the advantage of adjusting the pig's diet to its needs. If it is suffering from itchy skin, you'd know the quantity of oil you need to give.

Cons of Homemade Feed: A pig's diet should constitute of proper proportions of protein, oil/fat, carbs, vitamins/minerals, fiber, and water. You have to balance these in their diet and monitor their energy level, weight, and the skin or coat to see they are getting what they need. It's a time-consuming option to mix your own food. And if you choose to give them organic food, it would turn out more expensive than expected.

Poisonous Household Plants
If your piggie is going to live indoors, you need to know about poisonous house plants. Many common house plants are actually poisonous to animals and although many pigs might simply ignore house plants, some will attempt to eat anything.

More than 700 plant species contain toxins that may harm or be fatal to your pig, depending on the size of the pig and how much they may eat.

Therefore, it is especially important to be aware of household plants that could be toxic when you are sharing your home with a new pig.

Following is a short list of the more common household plants, what they look like and the different names they are known by. Several plants have several symptoms, especially look out for vomiting and diarrhea as a sign for you to analyze if it could be that your pig has eaten a plant. If so, either call your vet or a poisonous centre.

Aloe Plant: also known as *"medicine plant or Barbados aloe"*, is a very common succulent plant that is toxic to lots of animals. The toxic agent in this plant is Aloin.

Asparagus Fern: is also known as *"lace fern, emerald fern, emerald feather, sprengeri fern and plumosa fern"*. The toxic agent in this plant is sapogenin, which is a steroid found in a variety of plants.

Corn Plant: also known as *"ribbon plant, cornstalk plant, dragon tree and dracaena"*, is toxic to some animals. Saponin is the offensive chemical compound found in this plant.

Cyclamen: also known as *"Sowbread"*, is a pretty, flowering plant that, if eaten, can cause diarrhea, vomiting and increased salivation. If a pig eats a large amount of the plant's tubers, usually found underneath the soil at the root level, heart rhythm problems can occur, which may result in seizures or even death.

Dieffenbachia: also known as *"exotica, dumb cane and tropic snow"* contains a chemical that is a poisonous deterrent to animals. If a pig eats the plant, they will experience mouth irritation, especially on the tongue and lips that can lead to increased drooling, problems swallowing and vomiting.

Elephant Ear: also known as *"cape, caladium, malanga, pai, taro and via sori,"* contains a chemical which is similar to a chemical also found in dieffenbachia.

Heartleaf Philodendron: also known as "cordatum, split-leaf philodendron, fiddle leaf, fruit salad plant, horsehead philodendron, panda plant, red emerald, red princess, and saddle leaf", is a very common, easy-to-grow houseplant that contains a chemical irritating to the mouth, tongue and lips. An affected pig may also experience difficulty swallowing, vomiting and increased drooling.

Jade Plant: has many other names, including "baby jade, Chinese rubber plant, dwarf rubber plant, friendship tree, jade tree, or Japanese rubber plant". While exactly what is toxic to animals in this plant is unknown, a pig eating a Jade plant can suffer from loss of coordination and depression as well as a slowed heart rate.

Lilies: some plants of the lily family can be toxic to dogs. The peace lily (also known as Mauna Loa) is known to be toxic to animals. Eating the peace lily or calla lily can cause vomiting, irritation to the pig's tongue and lips, problems swallowing and increased drooling.

Satin Pothos: (silk pothos), if eaten by an animal, the plant may cause irritation to the mouth, lips and tongue, while the animal may also experience vomiting, difficulty swallowing and drooling.

The plants noted above are only a few of the more common household plants, and every conscientious pig guardian will want to educate themselves before bringing plants into the home that could be toxic to their canine companions.

Poison Proof Your Home
You can learn about many potentially toxic and poisonous sources both inside and outside your home by visiting the ASPCA Animal Poison Control Center website.

Always keep your veterinarian's emergency number in a place where you can quickly access it, as well as the Emergency Poison Control telephone number, in case you suspect that your pig may have been poisoned.

Knowing what to do if you suspect your pig may have been poisoned and being able to quickly contact the right people could save your pig's life.

If you keep toxic cleaning substances (including fertilizers, vermin or snail poisons and vehicle products) in your home, garage or garden shed, always keep them behind closed doors.

As well, keep any medications where your pig can never get to them, and seriously consider eliminating the use of any and all toxic products, for the health of both yourself, your family and your pigs/.

Garden Plants
Please note that there are also many outdoor plants that can be toxic or poisonous to your pig, therefore, always check what plants are growing in your garden and if any may be harmful, remove them or make certain that your pig cannot eat them.

Cornell University, Department of Animal Science lists many different categories of poisonous plants affecting animals, including house plants, flower garden plants, vegetable garden plants, plants found in swamps or moist areas, plants found in fields, trees and shrubs, plants found in wooded areas, and ornamental plants.

Animal Poison Control Centre
The ASPCA Animal Poison Control Center is staffed 24 hours a day, 365 days a year and is a valuable resource for learning about what plants are toxic and possibly poisonous to your pig.

a) USA Poison Emergency

Call: 1 (888) 426-4435

When calling the Poison Emergency number, your credit card may be charged with a $65. ((£39.42) consultation fee.

b) UK Poison Emergency

Call: 0800-213-6680 - Pet Poison Helpline (payable service)

Call: 0300 1234 999 - RSPCA

www.aspca.org = ASPCA Poison Control.

6) Toys and Recreation

Pigs <u>love</u> toys. They do irrespective of whether they are given indoors or outdoors. If it is a toy with food, it would be like a wish come true for them. Some favorites include old magazines, clothes and shoes, cat/dog toys, and infant toys.

Visit www.petsmart.com or www.pigstuff.com to find anything that you think they'd like. (Hint: Look for the Buster Cubes and Manna Balls.)

If you want to give them a toy that's not too noisy, too messy and still interactive, a rooting box can come in handy.

Again, remember to place your pet's safety first so don't invest in toys that are not heavy plastic or rubber. Mini pigs are extremely playful and would not only toss but also chew through the toys you give them.

7) What's the fuss for?

It's not a secret that a new parent remains anxious and tends to hover around their child, placing significance on every minor incident that occurs, trying to guess why he/she is crying, whether a cough was a hint to an impending flu etc. Being a foster parent can be even harder because it entails learning as well instead of pure reliance on one's instincts. To ensure you do not frighten your teacup – or vice versa – and that you do not go ahead and dump it, here are a few pointers that you can expect from them for as long as they are with you.

The belly rubs
One can never begin to show their affection to pets this way soon enough. They never seem to get tired of it and apparently it's second only to food in their list of enjoyments, which is exactly why some owners use it as a trick to control the amount of food they are given. Then again, you can use the opportunity to examine your baby for bumps and other injuries. No, this position will not let the pig assume dominance; it allows a stress free chance for you or the vet to trim your pet's feet, check tusks, clean ears, etc.

Why does it tremble?
It can be something as minor as a chilly wind that can be taken care of with a safely installed (heat) lamp or a warm blanket to cover the poor thing in. It can, however, be a symptom that your piggy is ill or in pain if somehow the lamp and/or the blankets are proving insufficient to keep it warm. At your end, you can note the temperature and observe if there has been any variation from the normal behavior to tell the vet about. A couple of reasons to have caused it can be abdominal pain and pneumonia so be on the alert against those. Other than that try to keep the windows, doors,

and hallways free of drafts to keep its sleeping area sufficiently warm. The ideal temperature for mini pigs is between 65 and 85 degrees.

Why does it itch?
Pigs are inclined to get lice. You can treat them for these large parasites with Ivermectin and clean up the place as well as any other pet or human (yourself included) that the pig has been in contact with recently. This can prevent re-infestation.

A second common reason for any pig to itch a lot is if it contracts mange, especially if it starts to shed. Ivermectin to the rescue once more. If it's a serious case, you may be looking at a more extensive treatment for your pig. [For further details, refer to the section under 'The Health Considerations'.]

However, if the medication doesn't seem to be working, then the vet may not rule out other likely possibilities such as insect bites or allergies.

Why does it suffer from hair loss?
It's quite normal for a potbelly to go through what is otherwise known as "blowing the coat".

Each pig can suffer from this at different times. Most will have it around June, others might sport a bald patch due to mud bathing. The thing is, it's there: the bristles can fall off in handfuls and from being fully-clothed, your pig can go completely bald before a new coat grows back. Another thing to note will be that some do not recover their appearance. They can continue to have strips and a general grungy look. So, it won't do to worry about it particularly as your pig ages.

Why does it raid the fridge?
This more often than not is a query by those who happen to offer treats to their pigs directly from their refrigerator. It can never be emphasized enough just how strong a motivator food is for these animals. They watch, they learn, and they replicate the action to help themselves. With no baby locks to deter them, they may

even try to move the fridge. Did you know a large pig can successfully tip over a fridge to open it? What's more, any tricks that owners attempt to eliminate the habit are easily and quite ingeniously thwarted.

Appeasing their appetite this way would result in an obese and unhealthy pig. Make sure you control it from the beginning!

Why does it grind its teeth?

This can be justified by several reasons. Your job is to figure out which one suits the situation best. First, it can be because the pig is losing its baby teeth. Second, pain can be a factor if it is accompanied by trembling as well. Plus, if the pig is not eating, a discomfort of a sort such as stomach issue or ear infection can also be an issue. Another thing would be stress or anxiety. This can be due to new visitors, travelling, etc. So, bond well.

Why does it shred fabric/paper?

It's normal for them, similar in nature to rooting. You cannot do anything about it except to accept it. But where the digging is related to search for roots, a spot to rest in or something to pass their time with, shredding is about making a bed out of anything they can get their hands – oops, teeth – on. So, whether it is a sheet off your bed, newspaper and magazines lying around, or dirty laundry, they will tear it up. While you may give the pig its own supply of old newspapers, towels, blankets, directories to root through, don't be surprised if your down comforter or exclusive draperies are ripped down to ribbons or if it takes up residence in your bed.

A word to the wise, some pigs tend to do it just for fun. You cannot blame them later for ruining your couch cushion because it apparently wasn't to their style or that they were bored. So unless you have a barn out there to shift them to or are willing to tone down what you have around, do not buy them.

Why does it bite?

A pig that is using its teeth to bite you can be seen as either spoiled or territorial.

Earlier it was mentioned that you do need to give them attention and affection when caring for them. Excess of anything is harmful and that stands true for personal attention to your pets. They become demanding and end up behaving like total brats, snapping at their owners when in pain or if their bed has been tampered with.

That being said, a (mini) pig's bite is not to be taken lightly. Make sure to keep their tusks trimmed. A tusk that is an inch long at least can lead to accidental stabbing, causing serious blood poisoning or other injuries. Let them blow off some steam by taking them for walks or letting them out in the yard for a while.

Why does it poop in the pool?
It brings to mind the 'classic' image of a pig lazing around in a muddy place and not quite the clean animal you have been sold. In contrast to this notion though, breeds like the kunkunes and potbellies are accustomed to having their droppings washed away by either rain or the stream they used to defecate in. Considering that, it seems natural for them to accept the pool you provide them with as effectively a version of a flush toilet.

Just make sure you are there to clean it frequently. Also, you'd need to place a smaller, tip-proof, tub as a receptacle for its drinking water; it might get dirty but at least it won't let water spill out.

8) The health considerations

A certified vet is without a doubt the best person in the situation to offer qualified advice for your pet's health problem. As a layman and first time owner of miniature pigs, it will be quite difficult for you to diagnose or treat the tiny one.

Plan ahead
It is a challenge to get your pig checked especially as they grow bigger with the passage of time. You need to have suitable transport to take them to the vet, that's for sure.

A few factors that may trouble you include:

- The 130 pounds of weight it carries now –both for you to lift him/her and for the car to bear
- Being ill and/or unable to walk
- Not accustomed to travel
- A lack of a crate or kennel that's able to support him/her during the journey
- Coming out of the vehicle at the building

It seems as if a suitable mode of transportation needs your due attention. It's a good idea too to teach a youngster how to walk up and down a ramp into and from the car. You'll remain safe from injuries and it will be easier on his joints as well.

Secondly, you'd have to be attuned to your pig's behavior to be able to coax him into the clinic because even sick pigs will try to make a quick getaway if they are scared.

Expenses
It's not only the food and bedding that's going to cost you money out of your pocket, but the routine and emergency care is something you'll need to deal with as well. They need vaccinations as per the vet's recommendations of course, the tusk trims, hoof trimming, deworming, etc. Ask the vet clinics in your area whether they are well equipped for treating mini pigs. Research and compare the cost of what these services might call for.

Obesity
The one major reason that kills most pigs is excessive weight in individual breeds. Their owners take it as something "cute", claim that it is in fact their love for the pet that compels them to feed them excessively and that they are better off than people who'd rather starve these miniature darlings.

To let a pig's belly touch and drag along the ground can cause abrasions. The improper diet, zero exercise, or pampering them to the extent that they manifest a complex network of blood vessels for every pound of fat that they take on is akin to a prolonged death sentence for them. The strain on the heart reduces their life span by almost half, in the due time of which it is likely to suffer from a poor quality of life. This is because most lose their ability to see and hear as well as develop arthritis; they turn snappy and nasty as well.

Believe me, you don't want one that's deaf, blind, and unable to shuffle more than a couple of feet before collapsing and gasping for breath. Furthermore, they cannot drink or eat themselves. You cannot love such a thing, there's pity yes for the 'unhappiness' that being trapped in their own body cause them, and revolt for the terrible smell that would eventually surround them because they won't let you near enough to clean or feed them.

Theirs are hard, dry and small droppings instead of the 'normal' firm, moist, and slightly larger ones. A proof like this alone should put you on high alert.

To raise a pig, you need to understand one fundamental fact: the creature is programmed to eat but it needs it in reasonable quantities only combined with exercise to live a healthy life.

So, for example, if you think daily walks round the block with treats is a good idea, you'd have to reconsider. It won't be long before the walk is unable to shed the excess pounds.

It helps though if you can spread food pellets over a large area to get the pig moving in search of its meal rather than just allow it to feed directly from the dish.

Remember the pig is no longer living in the wild but is dependent on you to provide it stimulation. Looking for food is one way to get them moving, working its mind on a task. Following this, you can attempt to cut back the fat clinging to his/her frame by (a) eliminating any and all junk food in the diet, and (b) reducing a little quantity even – not starve – until they can be deemed fit.

A third thing would be to stop believing that a treat ball would be a good idea because as stated earlier and emphasized repeatedly, mini pigs are NOT dumb animals. For something that you think will take energy rolling around to scour the pellets inside, a lot of them have been noted to take the ball to a corner and simply push it up against the fence or the wall so that the treats may drop out.

Therefore, plan for long-term and stick to it so that you have a pig that you can love and that can love you back.

Ulcers
Another common issue that mini pigs are treated for is ulcers. There are many reasons to cause these, the more prominent ones being medication, diet, and stress. What's more, they are interconnected.

In more cases than one, the mere knowledge that your baby doesn't eat anything and is showing signs of lethargy or depression for at least a day should throw up a red flag. If the miniature isn't eating its food, you can affirm a diagnosis for an ulcer especially if pressing the abdomen elicits squeals of pain. The pain would be because the stool would have turned harder on account of more moisture being absorbed as it passes slowly through the intestine.

You can also expect for the stool to be dark in color, sometimes along the blacker end, from the blood from the ulcer; a bright red color on the other hand should give you reason enough to suspect that it's not an ulcer but something else that's causing the problem since it's bleeding from the bowel.

For an ulcer that's developed either because of the lack of feed that he/she has been taking or because of the stress from the treatment of some other sickness, it's best to give ulcer medication like Famotadine, Carafate, or Omeeprazole. As an additional precaution, assign these for a different time of the day, following of course the vet's recommendations of frequency, dosage etc.

For constipation, give it food that has high fiber content as well as increasing the amount of water. Give them quality hay, treat them to a plain pumpkin pie or bran, flavor the water even if required to encourage them. There are hay pellets too that you can make use of only as a component of a rich diet. Besides these, a third fundamental to focus on would be exercise.

If these are ineffective, then you might as well order an enema to stimulate stool evacuation. Administration is not an easy task if you are not familiar with it and it is better to seek the help of the vet rather than risk injuries to your pet. But if the problem persists even after this, then it is more severe than first imagined.

Alternatively, do NOT administer the enema if you observe the pig vomiting. It is indicative of intestinal blockage or bowel stricture and the enema will only augment a problem that is already critical. A blockage has more chances to occur in pigs that not only vomit or do not poop but also have a lack of appetite and a tendency to tear up and chew on unsuitable items, especially the fabric or the plastic from their bedding.

In case the blockage has been a result of dry manure, they can be softened by the administration of fluids such as IV, SQ, or rectally; if it is the result of consuming a foreign object, it would make surgery mandatory.

Strictures, on the other hand, can cause rectal bleeding. It is normal for owners to fall for the symptoms that hint at poisoning; some may even put the pig down. Only physical tests such as a Barium X-ray can help determine a stricture. Once confirmed, the vet can run a variety of tests to determine the causes from Salmonella and Erysipelas to trauma apart from the constant need of monitoring color, size, etc.

This is to say that rectal bleeding is a red alert situation and has to be given due attention before you try to help the pig for the strain and bleeding it is suffering from during its bowel movement. Familiarize the vet with details like the diet he/she has been put on and the probability of access to toxic/foreign objects and let them do the job.

Mange
A disease that has maintained its status as a challenging pest to vets and owners alike, mange can be obvious, subtle, and sub-clinical. The sub-clinical category is a dangerous type for mini pigs to contract, as they become carriers with no visible symptoms.

Where others suffering from mange infestation will have dry and scaly skin (not including their normal dry skin condition), and will have white tracks on its body for every time it rubs against objects, the carrier will not. They won't even have the teary eyes, or the crusty, reddish-brown matter on the eyelashes and in corners, no excessive debris or smell coming from their ears and there will certainly be no scabs and/or tiny bumps under the surface of their skin or the orange coloring of the same.

It erupts suddenly for them when they are under unnecessary stress due to (a) coming of a new or losing a family member, (b) unexpected change in weather, (c) travelling to the vet or (d) if the gilt has not been de-sexed and is coming into the heat for the first time.

The condition turns chronic when left untreated. This time around, however, with additional signs like a thin coat, a thickened, scaly, and scabby skin, and/or for a black skin turning dark gray or otherwise exhibiting an orange cast, it is easier to identify and therefore treat.

Being wormed twice, or in some cases more than that for a given year, helps keep mange under control. To add to the worries, the damage to the skin and hair respectively can be mistaken for a result of inadequate intake of vitamins or improper diet whereas the change in temperament is simply a less common event to witness.

Since the ears are a favorite with these mites, it is important to treat them along with the rest of the body. According to one eminent Doctor of Veterinary Medicine, one way to confirm your diagnosis is to use a small melon baller to scrape deep in the ear to obtain some debris and skin; put that in a small, plastic petri dish, adding to it a teaspoon of baby oil. Leave it overnight to incubate at 37 °C. Any mites in there will be observed swimming in the oil the next day.

As a treatment then, you can prepare a solution that's ½ isopropyl alcohol and ½ hydrogen peroxide, warm it, and squirt directly into the ear, massaging the ear to loosen debris. Let the pig shake its head because it may help loosen the gunk too. The whole procedure and using Tresaderm to massage the ears afterwards should obviously be done under doctor's recommendation. Even then it won't be easy to deal with a pig who is objecting but it works especially when the pig gets a re-infestation more than once.

Consult with the vet too before you chose to use Ivomec Injection for Cattle and Swine, Ivomec Pour-on for cattle, or Dectomax. The luxury is useful when it comes to dealing with the occasional out-breaks from environmental conditions or exposure to an infested pig. However, if it's chronic, the mange has to be treated more aggressively.

The disease is not to be taken lightly since there have been cases too wherein severe mange led to a positive gram staph infection because of the constant rubbing and scratching of their skin. As a complication, the pig is unable to heal and requires a course of antibiotics as well.

Note: Be particular about weighing your mini pig before administering any med to it.

Back Injuries
It's an illusion really to think that your 'control' on the pig's weight is enough to save it from these medical issues.

While signs such as dragging of the hind toe, an unwillingness to walk, or walking sideways can let you figure out the problem, only the vet will be able to calculate the exact severity and hence the treatment upon examination of a paralyzed set of hind quarters, a twisted back, or the way it slopes when walking for example.

The course is likely to include dexamethasone injections, pain meds, and a sling to help it be mobile in order to avoid other associated problems. The issue with slings is that you need it in appropriate dimensions seeing how a narrow one can roll and slip while a wide padded one can become urine soaked – and consequently lead to scalding – if there isn't an opening provided. In addition, you need to be aware of its material as well to be on guard, checking it at minimum two times a day to ensure not only that it's still in place but that there are no pinched areas on the skin. If you leave the sling overtime, you are opening the pig up to nerve and tissue damage. Keeping the pig comfortable should be your priority at that moment.

Have good bedding and rubber mats at hand. Don't force the sling onto your pig. It will only make it panic or depressed. Play around with them before balancing and adjusting the sling around its body, offer it an old cushion to relax on. Keep them close to a heat lamp in winter to prevent flare-ups during the night. Just don't forget that the treatment needs weeks and months to work.

Lameness and Arthritis
Every once in a while a misstep, rough step and jumping from the furniture can lead to minor sprains, puncture wounds and even a bruise or fracture.

Where it's wise to take safety measures and discourage these jumps and provide ramps to ease movement etc, if you notice swelling or if your pig is shifting weight to a side or refusing to walk at all you may need to take it to a vet for an x-ray. A relevant question to expect at this stage would be the frequency of your pet's dilemma. This cannot be attributed to genetics alone. You have to take into account the aforementioned factors for lameness. A vet can interpret the location, the intensity, the cause, and as such the treatment to improve its life because it differs with the type of pig you own.

Akin to what we do for ourselves, a few medication/procedures have to be tested before you can claim to have found your pig a cure to this problem. In the meantime, continue your care by giving them proper beds, including if possible and if your pig likes it, rubber mats, comforter, a heat lamp, and ramps at different areas.

Bumps

There are several reasons your pig might have bumps on its skin. However, if it has more serious ones such as erysipelas it may need to be taken for treatment. It cannot be cured with a topical ointment. Your pig's temperature might rise to 105 even when there are no visible lesions for which it will need Pen-G injections immediately.

The point to make note of with this disease is that it requires treatment for around 5-7 days before switching to oral antibiotics. What's even more relevant is that the disease is notorious for killing weak or young pigs – the older ones barely survive either unless they have been given the right treatment at the right time.

Vaccination, although necessary, can take as long as six months. Complications include heart damage, sloughing of the skin, and arthritis. That is why you should contact your vet immediately once the disease has been identified.

Diarrhea

It's hard to imagine something like this for an adorable teacup that you wanted to play with. It's easy for them to contract diarrhea if their diet is not monitored. Where you can substitute the electrolytes and water by administering the same via injection, you'll need to contact a good vet to diagnose and help your pig. Make sure they are getting the desired quantity of fiber in their diet by feeding them wheat germ, pumpkin, bran, or oatmeal besides the regular quality hay and grass. You'd have to be patient while feeding them when they don't feel like it. Be careful though not to overdo your treatment as it may lead to constipation [see Ulcers]

Urinary Blockage

As we discussed before, it is important to have male pigs neutered before they can be kept as pets. What wasn't referred to was a common problem that it could cause, namely urinary blockages. This too requires emergency treatment.

The symptoms such as refusing to eat or favoring one hind leg may point to a back injury or lameness but if you see your pig straining to pass urine, hunching a lot or thrusting, and seems bloated, it means it is facing difficulty passing urine. At that moment, you'd better take your miniature to someplace such as fine sawdust in the toilet area to urinate and check it.

A better idea even is to test its pH with paper strips; the pig won't be worried about your 'odd' behavior as long as there's some sort of reward for standing still and letting you reach under the belly while he "goes". Additionally, you also have to be concerned for the test strip to not to touch anything apart from the urine itself, not the pig's body, neither the ground nor the air even, taking it out only just before you have to test. These are some rules that you have to follow in order to get an accurate result in terms of the color change. A pH that is slightly acidic, around 6-6.5, is considered appropriate; anything to the extreme at either end of the scale would be dangerous and aid in the formation of crystals causing this blockage.

Traditional medicinal therapy and massage (with mineral/baby oil and wearing doubled latex gloves) is always better to consult a vet before you self-diagnose and treat your breed for an affliction that might turn deadly later.

Salt Poisoning

For a pig that has not been held answerable when savoring delights in the form of pretzels and chips, and which did not receive adequate water, there's a high chance it can suffer from salt poisoning. This is because these animals cannot sweat out the salt and the cells in their body end up swelling as a result. If the brain cells are the ones affected, the aggravation can potentially cause brain damage and death. Seeking help in determining the severity of your individual case during the early stages only can have a positive affect.

Abscess
These usually crop up over the side of their face or on their jowl, and can result from tooth issues. However, a tumor can also be the culprit. A vet's consultation not only aids in diagnosis but also in the cause and reliable treatment for your pig.

One treatment that has often done the trick is to break it with hot packs while feeding the pig antibiotics referred by the doctor. The rather small, round and painless lump will first grow larger before a soft center forms over it that can be drained. Treatment isn't just an option in this case, even though it doesn't guarantee that the pet may not develop another one shortly. If it is related to a tooth problem, as a checkup can reveal, it may require a tooth extraction to keep it from invading the bone. If it does, that merely makes the treatment course more expensive and more complicated.

Uterine or Testicular Tumor
These are found abundantly in pigs that have not been neutered and the probability only increases as they grow older. This is why neutering them is a crucial part of your bargain in the first place because treating an adult pig costs more and has more dire consequences.

Roundworms
You don't necessarily have to own a sick pig for them to pass roundworms. Instead of experimenting with your pig, it's best if you have a vet ask about the best program for your pet. Deworming is not only meant for new arrivals but it should be done consistently. This is mainly due to the fact that your pig might not show any signs it has worms – even though unusual coughing is said to be one symptom – to warn you about the problem and that's why you have to respect the schedule.

Besides that, you can play your part by avoiding manure and muddy areas as well as changing the location of their feed every so often, i.e. if you are letting them consume treats directly off the ground. Pigs that eat in dirty conditions have greater chances of heavy infestation.

Eye Injuries

Eye injuries are common in pigs that love to root outside. A swollen eye can be taken care of with relatively mild ointments such as NeoPolyBac. However, a scratch would worsen if this were used to treat it. A vet's prescription can help.

Dippity Pig Syndrome

A deadly combination is to have young pigs, as old as two years max, stressed out in spring. Symptoms for this condition include blood oozing from the lines on their back. The lines, mostly running side to side, will be prominent and the pain the pig suffers from will be so bad it collapses, screaming, on the ground. Affected pigs may squeal when touched, the sensitivity raised especially around their rear end. They may exhibit a hunkered stance, distress, inability to use their back legs, and restlessness. It is not necessary for these symptoms to be exhibited all at once.

Besides reasoning with the inappropriate or a change in diet or water supply to experiencing a change in body temperature that might have caused him internal stress, the pig might also be prone to stress when out on a trip to the vet, having just changed homes, and/or routines, or by getting a taste of a violent thunderstorm.

Keeping their pigs in a quiet, darkened place have helped some of the owners but you need proper pain medication to soothe it. There isn't anything specific but some topical sprays or creams (1% hydrocortisone) can heal lesions/sores. You can also seek to control the stress levels with low music. Good hydration is also a plus point as you continue to reassure and comfort it. Other measures would be to apply Aloe Vera gel or other sunscreen to prevent sunburn and assist in healing of the lesions already present.

A complete recovery so far is as mysterious and spontaneous as its onset and has a probable duration of a day or two. It can be a once in a while event or there can be more than one attack. Plus, the vet can guide you with respect to anything else that can be done to make it more comfortable.

Other harmful diseases to be aware of
No matter how much you love your piggy, the law always looks at pigs as farm animals, even if you treat them as humans. This is why the government warns pig owners who keep them indoors against zoonotic diseases (diseases that can be passed on to humans and vice versa) and advises owners to make sure they always keep an eye for the symptoms. When there is an epidemic of diseases like swine fever and foot and mouth disease, even humans are at risk.

At times of an outbreak of such a deadly disease, even if the pig shows no obvious symptoms, it can be a potential carrier of the virus and a potential threat to the spread of the disease. Owners might only help spread the diseases further, unwittingly. There are some important things to keep in mind.

Exposing children to the threat of contracting such diseases is not justifiable for any parent. This is why there are strict laws regarding the adoption and registration of pigs all over the US and UK.

In the UK, the government is very strict about this and sometimes requires owners to obtain a pig-walking license to ensure that while taking the pig on a walk it is not a potential threat to the spread of diseases to other animals it might encounter. Usually, the spread of such diseases are via droplets and direct contact.

In Scotland, owners don't have the permission to walk their pigs. It is a strict and unalterable law.

If you have a farm with many miniature pigs, and one of them has contracted the fever or foot and mouth disease, then you need to make sure that the others don't get the contaminated food. Also, keep the pigs away from other livestock on the farm to prevent spread to other animals. You must notify the authorities to take the necessary action.

Arthritic Rhinitis
The symptom of this is usually a common cold or sinusitis. Any pet pig can contract this so you need to keep a close eye on your piglet, especially if you own more than one or have other pigs nearby. The good news though is that it is curable; all you need is a proper medication and a quick timely visit to the vet.

Usually, this disease transmits to piglets during the feeding process from the mother's teats. Otherwise, it can be transmittable via contact with an infected piglet. When the disease is bad, it can cause snorts and distortion of the nose.

Ringworms
This is a common problem seen in all species of pigs. When the pig develops this problem, symptoms include loss of hair and rashes on the skin, which takes the form of a ring. It itches badly, causing a lot of discomfort in the pig. It is a highly contagious disease, but with proper treatment, it is curable. You need to visit a vet without wasting time because it can spread to children in the house and to other pigs as well.

Salmonella
When your little piggy gets into the mess of another piggy, it is looking for trouble with Salmonella, which, when transmitted to human beings causes typhoid. This is also contractible when our food gets into contact with feces contaminated with this bacterium.

Nerve, Brain, and Spinal Disorder
Any of these disorders never end well in pigs, so you have to be watchful of symptoms of these problems. There are too many symptoms to list but they include lethargy, pacing around, strange noises, loss of appetite etc.

Pneumonia

Pneumonia is a bacterial infection and yes, your piglet is prone to having it when exposed to harsh weather and the causative agent. Miniature pigs often get it from their mom, but can also get it through contact with an infected pig. When this happens, it may become fatal if you don't take instant measures to get medical attention. The usual treatment is antibiotics. However, some preventive measures would do well in the first place.

Skin Disorders

Pigs easily develop skin disorders like dry and scaly skin when the weather is harsh. When you notice the signs, avoid frequent baths; instead wipe their body with a damp towel and get a prescription from the vet. There are moisturizing lotions that you can use to control the condition.

Skin Tumors

Although these are less common in miniature pigs, there are reported cases. You need to keep a close eye and get your piglet regular checkups to make sure you handle the problem in time if it manifests. The vet can easily perform a minor surgery and rid the pig of this painful condition. If you notice hair loss, shedding, scaling, and swelling, make sure you take it to the vet for examination.

Sunburn

Miniature pigs are extremely delicate. When exposed to harsh and prolonged sunlight, they get sunburnt easily. You need to make sure this doesn't happen in the first place, but if your piggy is a naughty one and sneaks out, then you need to get it medical attention without delay. If not, the piggy might get weak, lethargic, and even suffer from paralysis. Ultimately, ignoring the problem will cause its death. As soon as you notice skin burns, get a prescription from the vet to help heal the burns and apply sun blocker lotions in the piglet.

9) Safety

Where expenses to keep your pigs as healthy as possible are incumbent for you as its owner, so is taking the time – and dollars

– out of your pocket an important undertaking to keep it safe from danger.

As you fence the area, think of all the plausible things that can endanger your pig; think ahead in preventing rather than reacting later and being sorry. Use quality fences and not the lightweight chain link or welded garden wire to secure the pig's area. Obtain a good lock to place on the gate.

A pool provided to allow it to cool off should never be deep enough to make it drown. Therefore, put them to use appropriately; a child's plastic pool will do for the pig once it is fully-grown and becomes a good swimmer in time. Keep them off the in-ground pool if you have one at all costs because it can fall in and drown, especially in your absence.

Another thing to note with respect to water is that you can never give them pails of water to drink from because it's simply not in their nature to do that. They will be unable to drink from it if it is not a non-tip tub or dish. What they will be able to do however is to slip in headfirst and drown.

Keep naked electrical cords out of reach. In addition to being an electrocution hazard, it also has potential to strangle (if their curiosity got the better of them) and start a fire (if a playful tug brought down with it a heat lamp for instance). Secure all the cables in your home well.

Fourth, a harmless metal tin can become a source of toxic chemicals. The pig can bite through even plastic ones if they want to indulge in whatever it is you keep in there. Plus, it's not as if you have to forget a few of them lying around that would constitute a problem; leaving them 'protected' in the lower cabinets may not solve the problem. If you don't want it to suffer, store these well above their reach.

Similarly, toxic plants are something that you should be worried about when considering gardening. For example, ornamental plants and nightshade should be removed. Cleaning products, pesticides and such chemicals should also be kept out of harm's way.

Try to keep away heavy objects from them like ironing boards, ladders, tools and toolboxes. Check if there are any nails or splinters protruding from them, including what's used in the fencing.

It's not just the animals that you have to beware of when protecting your pig because apparently there are human predators too. They can be anyone from a person with whom you were involved in an argument recently to people who steal pigs to eat them. Not to make you paranoid or anything, but this is why it is advised that you ensure your pig's safety when you are not at home. By being safe, however, it does not imply that you keep it in an enclosed, poorly ventilated space and with no shade either. As a rule of thumb, remember if the place happens to be too cold or hot for you, it will be colder and hotter for your pig.

Yet another area to consider safety is transporting your pig whether it is a trip to the vet or taking it with you on a trip. To be concise, your pig is going to need secure crates, complete with a ratchet strap or zip ties, to be carried in. You cannot trust them in the back of your pickup truck without it. They can push it open; they can even break a window to get away from the moving vehicle. Install double gates in your trailer too.

Planning for breakdowns and traffic on the road is a good strategy while travelling with your pig. For one, it should never be under stress due to heat. If the car is especially a dark colored one, it is going to get unnecessarily hot, so much so that your pig can die before you reach your destination. Keep the car well ventilated, turn on the air conditioning, place ice cubes in a shallow pool to place it near him while keeping a check on the temperature with a remote thermometer. In addition to this, add in a couple of plastic cat litter jugs with extra water as well as a mister bottle in case of an emergency. For good measure, prefer transporting it at night.

Finally, for the safety of your pet, you have to place a few ground rules for your (or neighbor's) children and pets even if they are supervised around it. Ask the younger kids never to pick it off the ground, but to sit and let the pig climb into their lap to caress and cuddle with them. Since the kids would not have a firm grip, a frightened or shy pig may try to scramble loose from their arms, risking back injury or a broken limb in the process.

Moreover, a shove intended as a playful gesture can cause the pig to bite them by taking it for an aggressive action, which is exactly what older children may do to tease them. And it's not just the kids; some 'know-it-all' adults are found guilty of the same charge as well. If all your pig receives during its homecoming and making initial acquaintances is mishandling and improper treatment, it will find it hard to ever trust new people again.

The case is the same with other animals especially if there are dogs anywhere in the vicinity. If it's not yours to train, under **no** circumstances are you to leave your pig alone with that predator even if the two seem to get along in your presence. The dog can injure or kill the pig, and if the pig is large and has tusks, it can retaliate and do some damage of its own. If you try to skim over this issue, knowing that there are large dogs like a Rottweiler in your area and/or home, then you'd better be prepared to pay for extensive and repetitive surgeries to save a pig that's lost a hefty pound of muscles trying to protect itself.

10) The Training Classes

A grouchy pig is not a pleasant sight to see, the reasons being many. Narrow them down by answering the who, what, when, and how of the feeding schedule and menu. Second, consider the environment you are keeping your pig in. Does it have its own space? Does it have room for exercise? Does it feel threatened by somebody? Or is it unhappy with a quarrel in the family? It's not just the recent events that might be affecting it. Has it, for instance, been weaned earlier from its mother than usual? Or is it suffering from discomfort as a result of some illness? Physical factors aside, the point faring next on the list of priorities is the way your pig has been socialized, which is concerned primarily with the magic word: "discipline".

a) The importance of communication

Just as you normally are accustomed to doing, make use of both verbal and body language to express your ideas. You need to infuse in lots and lots of love to assure the pig that you care. Remember that pigs are more intelligent than an average pet; they are almost your equal. They therefore need to be presented with a positive outlook to reap the same.

It is very important that you always use its name whenever you are talking to him or her, especially while training them just as you would when following the sociolinguistic competence with a fellow being.

If you recall another basic to how their minds work, you can have the answer by putting two and two together: motivating them through food.

Since you are getting your micro pig to respond appropriately to your words, you'd need to repetitively drill it in them, both the words and the action together. For example, if you expect it to run to the door as soon as you say "Do you want to go out", then that's the phrase that you should be using when talking to it just before you open the door. Use them too even if the pig stands in front of the door and wishes to go out! The willingness of your pet and the frequency of your usage would decide how quickly he/she is able to pick your verbal and non-verbal cues.

For the Churchill quote to hold true in the instance, you have to be willing to leave the floor sometimes and learn to interpret what their sounds and gestures indicate about their concerns, needs, and joys. While each may have its own with respect to their personality, a common few are listed below to get you started.

SOUND/GESTURE	MEANING
Whining	He either (a) wants food; (b) someone's messing with him when he's not in the mood; (c) he *is* in a bad mood
Aroooooo	He is FAMISHED
Oink, oink, reeeeee	He is searching for something or someone and is consequently nervous A continuous oinking especially in the first few days to see if someone (preferably from the family) is around
A sort of purring/moaning sound	He is content [particularly while getting his belly scratched]
A sort of "woof"	He is warning you about danger [if it's a higher pitch] He is excited [if he's simultaneously running and playing around]
Ahhhh	He sees you as family and is greeting you
Lip smacking	He is clearly enjoying his food [if he has food stuck in his mouth] He is clearly angry and ready to fight; can also mean in heat if not castrated [if frothing at the mouth]
Screaming	He is mad. Reasons to be include confinement, hunger or could not find you

Tip #1: You need to use your intuition when dealing with your pet pig. Plus, for unacceptable behavior such as screaming, you have to take a firm stand and not give in or they'll continue the same for every time they need your attention.

Tip #2: Body postures shown by a pet pig are usually indicative of dominance levels. If your micro pig knows his position within the social hierarchy, flicking its ears, clicking jaws, and throwing back its head this can probably indicate an unhappy, challenged, or at most a spoiled pig.

b) The 5-minute program

It literally helps if you can just spend a few minutes of your day with your pig just so you can realize the dream of having a perfectly behaved little darling. In addition, a session that is longer than 3-5 minutes actually would bore your mini pig: they lose interest and frustration will discourage it from trying out something new.

If you fulfill the following quota, you will have a pig that will really respect you, remains calm and happy unless it falls ill or is injured. He will sit down and stay as you command, doing what you want it to do!

Make it creative and fun

It is no secret that stressful conditions supporting and not compromising effective learning and creativity is a myth of yesteryears.

As an intelligent animal, pigs are not immune to the effect this state tends to create. No one likes a harsh teacher and neither will your pig. Be empathetic to it and watch it swell with affection. If the training time is kept light and on the fun side of the things, your pig is going to look forward to spending those minutes with you, willing to please you. And after watching the enthusiastic reception and results, even you would like to train it.

The creativity mentioned above is to prevent the process from getting too monotonous for either of you to have any significant interest in it, especially once your baby has learnt the trick you wanted it to. Like a teacher preparing for her class, invest in time and energy, think of new tricks and research what others have accomplished; you and your pig will be happier for it.

Make a routine

As a constant trigger for repetitive learning in a natural way, you and your pig should have these sessions incorporated in their daily routines. Set the foundation and make sure the pig follows it. It will give you time to do other things.

To emphasize the power of everyday routines, the pig will begin to have a fair idea of their social role. This will allow them to actively participate in each session, gaining confidence and independence for every step it manages to do on its own. Akin to how we learn socially appropriate behavior through repeated exposure and successful and not-so-successful experiences, these structured exercises would give him another perspective to deal with the situation at hand, helping him learn the importance of two-way interaction wherein he's the initiator and you respond. Such flexibility additionally boosts their learning ability.

Since you are basically asking for a habit to be ingrained, take the opportunity to make them do a random exercise. Map out words for them and their respective meanings so that they understand better; the more they hear and see these together, the clearer their concept of something gets, particularly during active participation in the interaction. The timing is therefore crucial.

Be consistent

You have to be careful in being consistent if you want to communicate effectively with it. Using different words/phrases for the same behavior will confuse it, which is why everyone in your family needs to come to a mutual decision regarding how to respond every time the pig displays a certain action.

The variable, however, can be treated from a different angle, i.e. you do not avoid the trick time no matter what happens. It doesn't matter if you are tired or late for duty or have other people/work to attend to, the moment you know it's time, you should be there for your pig because it certainly will be waiting for your undivided attention.

A third position is your take on the standard you've set for it to achieve before you award it with a treat. You certainly cannot afford to be lenient on this one or the pig will get lazy and won't cooperate. If you want it to sit for fifteen seconds, then it will have to do that to gain the treat.

Be patient

Your pig won't learn it overnight, particularly if you only train for a few minutes at a time. Moreover, every trick differs with respect to the difficulty level (how naturally attuned they are to the suggested activity) and the motivation to learn it. For example, the pig can learn how to fetch a ball in a minute but may take as long as a couple of months to pick it up. But once they master it, you can be sure they won't forget it any time soon.

c) For an adopted/older mini pig

There are a number of perks to consider when it comes adopting an older mini pig as your family member. For one, an older pig, around two years, will have no shocking discoveries for you to uncover when it comes to size, as he/she will be nearly fully-grown. Apart from the size, they offer you a live experience and not just a sneak peak to their adult personality.

Third, most of the adoption committees and rescue homes are likely to offer older mini pigs a less pricey fee in places where the pet mini piglet is to cost you anywhere between $600 and $1200 or even more.

That being said, you must have a lifestyle that permits you to be a more devoted parent and a companion to your mini pig. Almost the same techniques are going to apply to educating an older pig. According to experienced professionals, there is a high probability that the pig will not appear as approachable or affectionate to begin with and so the owner might be hesitant in giving them the chance to "re-learn" their skills, which is wrong obviously.

Considering that their memories may be the reason they are hurting, give them due time to adjust to their new home, and do everything as you would do for a baby pig to earn its trust.

In order for it to see you as a companion, it is recommended that you do not just rely on food items to win their affection but rather that you proceed to general touching and petting, as well as the famous belly scratches, so as to eliminate an otherwise

81

frightening atmosphere. But remember not to make sudden moves around them; approach them slowly otherwise they might run away. Be patient. Let them come to you after a certain distance and when it does, get down on the ground at its eye level.

Take baby steps in teaching them. Be gentle and show it that you respect its boundaries, while making it abide by your house rules. This is a critical period because if you don't set these rules from the beginning only, the pig may become aggressive with time and may not take kindly to your training either. Observe them and get to know their personality so that you know how you can trick them into earning their food.

Don't fool yourself by thinking that it's a low maintenance pet. Having acquainted yourself with your pet through health and background records, you have to make the placement area a good, if not perfect, match for the pig to thrive in especially with the stress of a sudden transition. In case the pig was being kept in a destructive setting, like for example being caged indoors, your pet might prefer a different setup and expect that you will teach it appropriate manners and housebreaking skills that the previous owners had not necessitated. What's important on your part too is your ability to generate a similar environment as the previous home had provided (if it was a positive one). This includes preparing an outdoor area if you are buying/adopting an outdoor pig.

d) For pigs displaying bad behavior
You cannot dismiss it. The more disgracefully it behaves, the greater your form of punishment should be. And it has to be immediate. If the pig has attempted to bite your hand – pig bites are very dangerous – while you are giving them a treat, a loud "NO!" or any other negatives that you have taught them can surprise them. But it won't be effective alone in this case. Try ignoring them or giving them a light push.

Once you have scolded your pig, use the "time out technique" to instill the severity of this action in them. Isolate them for a quarter or half an hour in their room. Tell them they have been bad. Tell them you didn't expect such behavior from them and nor will you do so in future. Once the time has passed, go back to check on them. Refrain from giving them treats or patting their back just now or the session is going to lose its significance. They can have them both later when they are on their best behavior again. If, however, a similar bad behavior on their part caught your attention again, then it is back to a time out session, devoid of normal activities.

To make it work, remain consistent with the actions and words so that the pig can understand the implications.

However, most people who believe that having taught their pig the meaning and thereby the restrictions set by "no" is a commendable achievement on their part have never been more wrong. They are in fact offering the pig the ideal situation to establish dominance. Therefore, if you are to observe these households, you will get to know that the pigs set the majority of the rules. What's more, to him, the word "no" is simply ineffective, implying only that an activity is not to be attempted as long as someone is watching him.

An owner who finds it easier to lock him away when there are visitors than to teach him positive regard for others outside the immediate circle is not taking the commitment to owning a pet pig seriously. Not taught their place in the hierarchal order, the pig is more dangerous at these moments when the sense of fear displayed by the 'stranger' makes him more aggressive.

As a rule then, no member among your family or friends should be afraid of your miniature pig; the weaker and more afraid they are, the greater their chances of being targeted. It is said that about 75% of pig problems are because the people in charge of it have not responded to its advances in the correct way for at least the first six months or so. Maybe they would have done so had they known that just standing up to it would be enough in controlling the aggressive behavior and would not require any correction.

Don't forget that these pigs are highly intelligent and can engage in a fight they know they'll win to resolve the dominance issue. Knowing that your pig will be testing you, observing your reaction, calculating its opportunity, and waiting until you respond, you have to have several methods to waylay it.

With loud verbal reprimands, you will be insinuating that commands given loudly only have significant value. Another problem can be that they make the pig afraid of loud noises or alternatively it may frighten other people enough to make them afraid of the pig.

Secondly, while squirt bottles and newspapers have been successful in more cases than one, the fact that you won't have these items on you for immediate correction undermines their importance for a pig that is biting, lunging, snapping and jumping.

So, without getting into a fight, hurting, or frightening your pig, seek to positively establish yourself as the boss even as you are taking away their privileges at the time they demonstrate bad behavior. You can use the following technique when making the correction.

Learn the aggressive signs that your individual pig displays so that you are prepared when you see it coming. You have to quickly grab its mouth and hold it closed, not allowing him to run away or swing its head. In the first few attempts, you can pet the pig to set him up into a comfortable position for you to hold his mouth closed without hesitation and without having to chase it around the room, trying not to pull back if he snaps. You can also wear a leather glove but then again since it's not going to be near you at any given moment that the pig chose to get aggressive, you have to ensure that by the time you master the technique, you have overcome this little fear of yours.

Hold it in the position for 2-3 seconds and release but not before telling it off with a firm no. The surprisingly short time duration is meant to secure you a victorious control of your pig without

84

being involved in a wrestling match with it. On average, it takes four to six times of repetitive handling for two-three seconds until the pig becomes comfortable. Remember, there is to be no display of emotion either during that period and you may follow it up with your normal routine.

To make your pig obey, you have to make it compatible with the severity of the situation with time, i.e. more time for more severe actions. If you are going too fast for your pig to understand this correction and wish to remain in total control, back off a bit.

As soon as you reach this level though, you'd need to lift him off the front pig and make sure its mouth is closed. This you can do by using both hands to cover its mouth by placing one hand on the leg that's near the shoulder and one on its mouth. A third option to resort to if your pig is wearing a harness is to keep one hand on the harness and the other on its mouth. The time duration for this exercise is five seconds that should go onto twenty once in the same manner.

Once you have verified that the pig understands it, you can include the next phase namely to drive him backwards for approximately a foot while its front feet are off the ground. Again, the push for each correction is to take him further across the room until there is a wall or a piece of furniture against his back. This may seem impossible in theory but it is possible practically.

The last of these steps is to make the pig sit and stay. This is one reason why "sit" is often a priority in the list of mini pigs' training. Always remember to release him when done to prevent it from wandering.

In order to pull off a successful correction, you have to take into account factors like how long your pet has continued to bite, the frequency of the correction it has received, and the effectiveness of those corrections, besides the obvious consistency and follow up in relation to the aggressive behavior.

e) What are these rules essentially?

So, you are now familiar with the tools you need and the training fundamentals you must adhere to, but you still don't have a clue as to what purpose they can serve you on a daily basis. For each behavior that your pig adopts, knowing what you want should be at its forefront. This is an important factor so that you don't second-guess yourself and just accept whatever you are getting in return. If the animal is showing improvement and is progressing well, you can raise the bar in the end to improve the behavior even more.

In planning activities and tricks, make sure everyone on board is clear about what needs to be reinforced and what can be expected from the pig to make it form connections on its own. You can take some time and focus on another behavior but it will quickly come to understand what reaction would make you end the training session quickly so they are going to adopt them specifically for other behavior too. Generally, you can ask for specific behavior three times at least, expecting to pull off the right interaction if the signal and the setup is in complete harmony; if not, you may leave the behavior at the moment and come back to it later.

f) Target training

One way to have fun while communicating with your pet pig is to use a versatile training aid as a target that he would have to touch for a treat. The best thing about it is that you are free to use any object for it as long as it is a solid thing. A clicker for one does great when you want to discipline your baby by telling him where and how to do something, for example, moving towards the ramp or your hand in a specific way. Instead of trying to manipulate him and ruin your relationship, you'll be able to achieve your target easily by giving him a choice to participate.

How does it Work?

You teach the pig to touch and follow the stick's tip to the desired place. When he does it freely, you can lead it wherever you want without having to pull, push, coax, or lift. Where normal everyday tasks like getting into the travel crate will be simplified using this, it has also been found useful when it comes to teaching your pet tricks like retrieving of an object, closing a door, or turning off a light switch.

What Do You Need to Do?

Keep the target stick in front of the pig so that they can see it and are able to touch it when you command them. When it does, reinforce it positively – "good" – keeping a pleasant tone and Cheerio pieces as a reward. Keep the sessions short and while patience is the key, it is important that each of them ends on a successful note so begin with small movements and then the difficult ones whether it is to make it bow down to reach the floor for touching the tip of the stick or playing a piano with his nose.

Alternatively you can train a pig with an imaginary target. Once your pig has learned the behavior, he'd no longer require a target as motivation to perform it correctly and without hesitation. Where earlier the pig had to make that mental leap to coordinate the cues before him and figure out what the trainer wants, he'd be able to do it spontaneously later on because frequent repetitions have helped ingrain the anticipated behavior for him. However, a lot of exposure to the same behavior, as elaborated by experienced trainers, is a problem when training your pig because it would make their interaction more predictable and less interesting from the perspective of both the parties. Thus, it needs to be carefully used.

There has to be some means of communication that would tip off the pig that he's achieved his target and can expect a treat for doing it properly. An appropriate form of this can be a whistle.

For example, when you instruct a pig to make a circle, you can sound off the whistle at the peak of the behavior so that the animal returning can look forward to receiving an appreciative pat on the back as well as delicious treats.

You have to ensure that the pig understands that the treat is not for just returning to you. That's when a bridge signal is used, for example, for a sequence of behaviors, it would have to apply to all instead of the individual event.

What's the reward?

Anything that your pet likes so much that he would readily repeat the behavior in future; you may want to use it as a reward to reinforce your training. Generally, most people assume that has to be something along the lines of toys and food. However, if you think your pet merely loves your voice and presence, or would benefit from a healthy game after a session, you can surprise him with it. Plus, the motivation is likely to vary with passing time for any one stimulus so it is better to have a couple of them up your sleeve that you think would work at any given time for the desired outcome. And yes, it is important for you to reward only when he has met the criterion a hundred percent.

It is important that you begin with primary reinforcements like food, water, or provisions of shade or warmth for innate needs when in the primary stages of your relationship; others like the sounds or other forms (secondary reinforcers) that your piggy enjoys should come afterwards. And while these "positive" reinforcements, i.e. to adding something that holds value for the pig to its environment, is preferred, you can retain control via negative reinforcement, which for instance can be to remove the board once the pig has walked up the ramp. As far as training for mini pigs go, you have to be familiar with how each behavior has been received by their breeds before so as to know their limits and be able to challenge them respectively.

g) Simple tricks for your mini pig

We all love a pet that can perform these sets of tricks perfectly and even though to see a mini pig doing the following would make it hard for you to resist showering him with treats, you'd rather teach it to them sooner than later only because the latter will be practically impossible.

Training the pig to sit

The following is the way most owners have found to work for them when they want the micro to sit on their command. By holding a treat in their hand right above the pig's snout, they would kneel in front of them and simultaneously say "Sit, [pig's name]". Some also used to gently push them on their lower back until they would sit. When the pig sat down, they'd be rewarded with the respective treat, patted on the head, and given verbal praise. It's imperative that you repeat the process a couple of times before the pig learns to connect the signifier with the signified. Hide the treat in your hand and get them to sit by just saying, "sit". To emphasize, you can give another treat when they get up. But supposing that your pig does not sit down when you move the treat backwards towards its ears and eyes, but moreover begins to trot backwards, you should take him to a corner and try again. With nowhere to run to avoid training, the pig will sit down and tilt the head to see the treat.

Training the pig to wave
Make your pig sit down and then, holding the treat in one hand, say "wave" and use the other hand for the signal. You may also reach down and softly tap the back of their front leg. Give him the treat the first time he even lifts it a little. Beginning from the easier upside down wave, you can later modify these to mimic as if you are actually waving at him. Repeat it in the morning as well as at night.

Training the pig to spin
Some may call it teaching a pig to circle but it's one of the easiest tricks to teach them. Let them follow a treat until he completes the circle. Once he does, emphasize the action by saying the word "spin" and then allowing him to have his treat. On the other hand, you can save the treat as the consolation prize and get him to spin just by giving the hand signal as well as saying the word.

Training the pig for the litter box
The best thing about having a miniature pig is that you'll only need to clean up one spot after them since they'll be using the same place every time for this purpose.

If, however, that is not where you want them to go the toilet, you'd need to tell them that properly. Having a place alone will not serve your purpose, especially for the piglets who are less than six months old and do not have full control over their bowels.

[**Note**: Don't use a litter box that's made by clumping cat litter or cedar shavings. The former tend to cause internal damage to your micro pig if it ends up eating it – as has been commonly observed – while the latter will release horrible oils.]

You'll note that the piglets will initially, as instinctively clean animals, use a particular corner of their room that is opposite to and at a fair distance from their bed and food/water bowls. One suggestion for new owners is to keep them in a small place, approximately of a 5 x 5" area, until they are completely litter trained. Even for the younger ones, it's important that you keep them close to a litter box and lead them towards it every two hours or so.

Place the litter box in the corner that you'd want him to use. Make sure that the box is shallow enough for him to easily get in and out of. Add pine shavings or unscented, non-clumping kitty litter. During training, keep some droppings in the litter pan. You'd need to do this even while cleaning the tray until your piglet is able to recognize the spot as his new toilet. While this is a temporary measure to make the pig aware of its bathroom area, it is advised that you do not use strong and odor neutralizing detergents to clean the pan or else the miniature pig won't use it. If it relieves itself outside the box it will return to the same spot.

Choose a phrase to use whenever you are taking them out of their crate in the beginning. You can say "go potty" and remember to praise them by saying "good piggy" as soon as they do.

Since you are building a habit, you can instruct them over time by taking them out to potty (a) as soon as they wake up; (b) every 2-3 hours of the day; (c) when they've finished eating their food; and (d) before putting them to bed.

Don't harm your micro pig if there are any accidents during or after learning. This will only make it scared of you.

Training the pig to fetch
For this purpose, you can begin with playful items like a ball and Frisbee that you can tape a food item to. Allow them to smell it first before you throw it. In most cases, the pig will successfully run after it. When he does, you can go to him and give him some food. Repeat for a number of turns. After that wait to see him coming to you for food every time he's able to fetch the item.

Training the pig to beg
Some people find it cute to see their mini pigs sitting on their hindquarters and 'begging' them. If you are one of them, you should know that the activity in itself is difficult for the pig to achieve. What they can do, however, is to lift their feet at the front into the air for a little while. And what can be a better motivator than food to have their feet come off the ground? Simply hold it above their head, succumbing to their fascination only when they have their feet in the air.

Remember that you can continue to increase the time slowly and gradually.

Training the pig to not chew household items
Wouldn't you look around for something to do/something to *feed* your intelligence with if you had nothing to do to pass your time? Well, your new best friend does the same as well. He cannot help but explore and forage around to avoid boredom if he can.

In accepting this, you need to provide the respectable means that you want your pig to occupy himself while you are not available. It's common to hear other pig owners complaining about how their Pot Belly has turned the place upside down, how he's always getting into mischief etc. The fault is not with the pet, which is just trying to make his or her own fun. The problem is with the owner who gives them too much freedom and not reliable toys to play around with.

91

If you are considering stuffed animals, you'd not only have to opt for a low or no-stuffing one, but teach him how to use these objects. Otherwise, they'll just pull out the toy stuffing and eat it, especially when unattended.

It's better though that you find an enjoyable pass time that the whole family could be a part of. For the time that he would be alone, you have to tell him which objects are forbidden for him. So, whenever you do find him anywhere near those items or playing with it, make sure you assume the position of the lead pig and reprimand strongly. It is important that you catch him in the act and not when you are coming to a "scavenged" home because the latter would cause confusion.

Use instructions like "No, leave it" as you take him away. A favorite way to not risk tantrums and/or effectively divert attention would be to give them their favorite toy quickly. These can be anything from a (large, shallow, wooden/plastic) rooting box filled with birdseed or river rocks, a soft chew toy, or a small/medium sized ball that you've bought or made for him. Praise him as he accepts it.

If you allow him to shred magazines or newspapers, you'd have to follow a similar pattern to ensuring that he is attentive to only those that you provide. The rest of them would have to be kept pig-proof as well, i.e. kept out of reach like the dangerous candy, household cleaners, etc.

Training the pig to shake hands
Want to tell your neighbors what a friendly pet you are being a daddy/mommy to? Teach your baby this trick. Kneel in front of them and gently lift his right leg with your right hand while holding a treat in your left. Don't let go immediately. Say "shake hands" and shake their leg. After that give them the treat and say "good piggy". When you believe you've repeated this exercise a good amount of times, you can try holding out your hand asking for a handshake and wait until he lifts his hoof and places it on your hand. As delighted as you might be at that moment, don't

forget, you'd have to give him the treat even then *and* praise him as well.

Training the pig to follow you
Let the little guy smell the treat in your hand while you stand in front of them. Say "come on piggy" and let him follow you for at least two meters before you give him the reward. Continue this way, each time taking a longer route until you give him another treat. Once mastered, the piglet would follow you with just a "come on piggy" without necessitating you to have a treat.

Training the pig to swim
Raising a pig as a pet necessitates that you provide at least a child's swimming pool for him to play in when it's hot outside. Splashing in water is the only way they can keep cool. However, they may be afraid to step into a pool initially. Where cutting a "doorway" in a side and coaxing your pig with a few apple chunks or grapes may help him to step in, you have to teach them a few basics to make sure they don't drown if they have chosen to jump into one.

You have to be close by as you let it wade in the shallow water. Don't throw him into water and don't let him over do it. As great an exercise as swimming may be for them, there is a possibility that he may get tired. Help them get out of the water and direct them to use the pool steps in the process if it's no problem.

Training the pig for transportation
It's the least you can do besides the ear scratches and belly rubs to ease discomfort. Indeed, going to a vet or your sibling's home shouldn't become a problem now that you've got yourself a new pet, and you should train your pig for the crate.

First things first, you should let him get used to the crate you'll be using. It will also give you a fair idea of if the crate is big enough for the pig to stand in there comfortably and also to move around a few paces. In doing so, you let him have a practice time for being in the crate uninterrupted, beginning from a few minutes every day and going for a similar number of hours that you'll be travelling before you make the trip.

Next, you'd have to make your pig used to your car just so that it won't freak out at the time for that either. Before a consecutively long drive, you ought to go on a small one with him secured in the back of the car in the crate for safety to see how well he is holding on. Note the maximum time that he can go to determine when you'd better stop to give him a snack, a bathroom break and a walk otherwise.

Your pig would need plenty of cool air so make sure the vehicle's air conditioning is not only in perfect working condition for you but the cooling should reach the back seat for your miniature in the crate. He'd also need to remain hydrated especially during summers, so make sure you have a car properly equipped for that. As unappealing as a carsick potbelly may sound, it's something you'd have to deal with so have your car ready for all sorts of emergencies.

For unloading, you can use a small aluminum ladder or build a small ramp to let it slide out of the crate.

[**Note:** If you believe that you'd be travelling outside of your respective state, then you should check the regulations – for USA residents, that will be the USDA – for the ones that you'd be entering/going across. They are different for different states and because mini pigs, despite being pets, are able to transmit the same diseases as swine, you cannot risk not taking a copy of his recent Health Certificate with you. Some of them may require blood testing as well.]

11) Raising a Pig Family

Pigs are by nature herd animals. Whether it was this general information or a probability that you found yours adorable and thought of having a little family running around your house, it is not out-of-the-ordinary if you are actually considering raising multiple mini pigs.

The point of concern, however, arises when you think it natural for them to settle together happily. As you'll find out later, in pairs or in groups, their yard-time experience (socialization and bonding) may differ from your expectations.

a) Hierarchal issues
In running in and out of your house, they'll always be squabbling and testing to see if they could have their position changed. From minor to turning rough and ugly, especially with a new one and not of the same litter, there's nothing predictable about it.

b) Individuality
Add to it the fact that every pig, much like us, will have a different personality. Mostly, it is the first one that gets to bond with you the most. They can be whiney, might prefer to be outside for most of the time and complain at the idea of possible confinement. They may get along with the rest of the pigs while shying away at the approach of other people or be cuddly with you or may not get along well with the other pigs!

c) Socialization
Remember, it is important for you to focus on socializing your pig from the very beginning. And for that very matter you were initially advised to choose your pig from a breeder who specializes in training them for it.

Once you have the miniature at your place, you can improve on it but you have to be very patient for your efforts to bear fruit. You have to let them get used to the new space, their home/territory that you have restrained them to when you cannot supervise their exploring.

Give them a treat – not a Cheerio but a food pellet that they can recognize – when they seem a little more comfortable around you. Praise them when they take it from you. Take care not to scare them away by trying to reach out and touch them in these early stages. A little more contact, a little more exposure to you each day will do wonders and make their journey from wild to social a bit easier.

Introducing to other pets

If you have other animals about, it is your responsibility to initiate an understanding of some sort between them and your mini pig. Since pigs are prey animals, you should allow your pets to have contact with them from behind a gate. Cats can get along with them but not dogs. But that's just a generalization. Even horses, donkeys and the like can break the neck of a pig while people who keep theirs with chickens and goats rarely have issues with them.

NEVER leave your pig alone with other animals though.

d) How are two pigs better than one?

This is a very good option indeed to consider if you have children at home. The pig knows a child is not the top hog and would challenge one to see if they can move up the ladder towards the status.

Adopting a second one can give it a playmate it can direct its attention to; they'll play together, sleep and be warm together. This especially holds true if you are in a colder climate – together they'll fall asleep in a pile to stay warm and never feel lonely especially if you don't have time for them. In plain words, the second pig can help you fulfill the emotional need of the first one that you cannot provide them.

e) Double trouble?

Most pigs however resent other pigs and want to be your only child. They'll bicker, if not fight, when sleeping to imply they are 'tolerating' each other. On the other hand, some even have fits and will attack one another on sight given that their gates were open.

Getting them at the same time, and as babies, can waylay stress as well as reduce the chances of them trying to dominate one another, although even that may not guarantee it. They still need both your love *and* attention.

Suppose you wish to provide a companion for your lone pig. You have evaluated the earlier propositions of space and expenses of having another one in your home, discussed it with other family members and are ready to make the necessary adjustments.

f) Other factors
These include size and attitude. For one, it is always better to have a second pig that's roughly of a similar size and shape as the pig you currently own. True, you cannot confirm how big your miniature is going to be. But a pig that's of the same breed and of the same size at the given age will not prove to be otherwise. As you will come to note, there will be less of the dominance game and, if need be, they will be able to take care and defend themselves from the aggressive one relatively easily. On the other hand, a larger one would, not once but several times, try to get a smaller one or a baby cornered. The latter won't be able to get away quickly and may suffer injuries in the process.

Plus, since you want them to share a pen eventually, it is good if you prioritize and observe the attitude of the pig you are going to buy to give the older one company. It is important that they feel good together. Think about your pig's temperament and buy one whose nature you think it would be compatible with.

For example, if yours displays an aggressive attitude, you might not want to encourage that by getting another such pig. A pig that isn't aggressive but capable of defending itself would be perfect. It is also possible that the latter would dominate and influence the other pig to not be so aggressive.

You might not want an aggressive pig at all; if the current pig is not aggressive at all, then a newer one that is would be getting into fights frequently to get his/her space. In this case, it would be ideal if you brought them a younger companion.

g) Introducing the second pig
For the first few weeks, you might want to keep them separated or under strict supervision. If you have them restricted to your house, you should invest in a baby gate to fence contact simply

because the slower you take this, the less chance you give them to be violent at their first real meeting. A fence would break the ice and get them used to each other, even if they remain obstinate and may not completely accept it.

When you believe they are ready for a proper introduction, bring them together for a very short period. You can obviously increase the exposure with the passage of time. Avoid giving one an edge above the other by having them on a neutral territory, neutral to both of them so they are not worried about defending their place. Avoid introducing them within your house because that may result in broken items and injuries.

Nevertheless, be prepared to break them up if fighting ensues from the meeting. One way to do this is to have them on a harness and lead, which will allow you more control. If you forget to do this, a second way to separate them would be to use the lid off the garbage can or a smooth board that you can put between their heads and sort/separate them. You are not advised to use your hands or legs to break them up as they can make a mistake and end up hurting/biting you, which may lead to an infection.

A point to remember in this case is that this is a natural process so you cannot, should not really, give them rewards for being good or bad for this matter. They have to have one dominating the other. If the fighting only results in a few scrapes and cuts rather than ripped ears or cut lips, then you've certainly done your job. Keep monitoring the interaction until one retreats because that indicates the fight is almost over.

Don't hit your pig at this time if their attitude is making you angry. The most you'd get anyway is them tolerating each other. Treat the scratches and arrange for separate accommodation if you think it's necessary. Call a vet if they have incurred more serious injuries. Both you and the doctor have to examine it properly because pigs can heal quickly; you must make sure that they wound has in fact healed from the inside out.

Keep them together in this or some other neutral space for a few days before returning them to the pen together. This will allow them to sort out the relationship, with one being submissive and the other dominant at their own convenience and comfort.

As a precautionary measure, do not introduce one to another if any one of them has tusks or they would have injuries of a more serious kind. Trim them first.

[**Note:** Neutered pigs are said to be less troublesome regardless of gender.]

12) Mating and reproduction

Naturally – or luckily –you hadn't gotten around to neutering your little baby since purchase, and you still have a chance of raising a family. It is important then that you do not ruin this.

If you wish for a wonderful friend as curious, happy, and amusing as pig pets make, then finding them a mate is the thing to do.

Research the sire or gilt first to know prior to mating the possible characteristics and traits that can be passed to their piglets. A complete history and health records can be compared for both of them too.

To know what the vet or the breeder is referring to, a few terms to remember them by in this case are defined in the following table.

Terms	Definition
Barrow	A male piglet that's neutered before maturity
Boar	A mature, unaltered male
Dystocia	Abnormal labor
Estrous Cycle	A phase of the female's sexual cycle
Gilt	A female that never had a litter
Sow	A female that has given birth to a litter
Stag	A male pig that's neutered after maturing

It was mentioned earlier that boars that are not neutered between 4-8 weeks of age would take just 52 days to become fertile. Breeding is the only thing they are capable of thinking at the time besides food as displayed by how they'd mount just anything – logs, bales of hay, your legs. They emit a very strong odor. In addition to this, what you must be familiar with is that they are very protective of their females so you have to be very careful around them.

Females come into heat every 21 days if they have not been spayed by the time they are about 16 weeks. Their vulva will start swelling and turn reddish, and they'll even try to mount other females! In the meantime, it can become nippy and attempt to burst out of their pens to search for boars.

It is recommended that you wait for a few months longer than the first time that your pigs come into heat and avoid mating when they are young as that would result in either squashed piglets or a sow that is not able to feed the piglets. Paying attention to the time the female comes into heat is another crucial point that you should be paying attention to so as to offer them the best chance of becoming impregnated.

Pregnancy or gestation lasts approximately for as long as 114 days. A few days before or after parturition a thin, yellow fluid is secreted by the mammary gland. For the first time that gilts give birth to a litter, they may be a few days early. On average, the litter size remains 6-8; it can exceed to be 12-15 too. It is a good idea to take the sow for a checkup to check on the progress of its pregnancy. A sonogram can show you the number of piglets it will bear so you can make appropriate arrangements in time as well. It will also be able to forewarn both you and the vet of potential problems.

You might want to have a farrowing/gestation area ready as the days get closer. It should be long and narrow in dimensions, big enough and strong too to accommodate both the sow as well as the expected litter. They must be able to lie down, stretch, and sleep there.

Is your sow ready to give birth?

You can tell your pig is pregnant if she does not get into heat at her normal time. If you are unable to determine as to how far along she is into her pregnancy – the gestation period is roughly for 3 months, 3 weeks, 3 days – you may get the vet to perform an ultrasound so you can keep a record.

The vulva swells when there are only 4-5 days remaining to birth; earlier than that, the belly will get bigger and the teats will start dragging on the ground. This is when the restlessness and nesting would begin.

They are not unlike other mammals in this case. Quite basically, you'll be able to spot her acting oddly. She'll even bite if disturbed when she's at the "nest" she's created for the time.

It will be okay for you to approach her once she lies down on her side and becomes self-absorbed. You have to be gentle and soothing, moving slowly, and just staying away from her head.

It is a messy business. So while you may be wearing clothes that you won't mind getting ruined, you have to have towels, rubber gloves, scissors, and water available if you are planning to do it yourself. Keep a shallow pan of cool water for the sow besides a bucket of warm water to wash yourself off.

Normally, it's the feet of the piglet that will come out first. Eventually, each piglet will be delivered in its own sack and you'd have to pull that away from the piglet. Or it may be that the sac has dried and completely covered the piglet. They won't be able to open their eyes completely after birth and this should be your cue to gently remove it using warm water. It will be transparent but you would be able to identify it because of its dried-skin texture.

If the baby's head is soft to touch and gives no scaly feeling, then you can see that unlike a cat's or dog's litter, baby pigs are born with their eyes open and functioning. You'd need to give him time to adjust his hearing and smelling.

Use a towel to rub it briskly and get the lungs to function. Use an aspirator if the situation demands it. With the sack off and the mucus cleaned away, you can take some string, tie the umbilical cord and cut the rest away.

You are NOT to put the piglets and the sow together until the latter has given birth to all of them. Only then are you to encourage the piglets to suckle.

Complicated Delivery
Where an uncomplicated delivery may take around one to two hours to complete, with babies weighing less than a pound, it can be prolonged and the female pig may strain to give birth.

Signs to indicate that veterinary assistance is required include:

• It's been more than 115 days in gestation
• No pigs delivered despite straining
• A decaying placenta or foul discharge
• Extended interval (more than half hour) between the birth of piglets
• Labored breathing, inability to rise, and weakness as the due date closes

Stillbirth
Like other animals, mini pigs can have stillbirths as well. One cannot completely prevent it. However, you might want to look into some reasons that can cause some.
• The mother wasn't being fed properly
• The piglet had a genetic defect
• The piglet was infected with some disease or sickness while still in the womb

You can help prevent it by getting together pigs that are not related closely and that come from good stock. In addition, make sure that both of them are in good health and carry no symptoms of any disease. Take them for their shots before copulation. When

102

the gilt gets pregnant, feed her high quality feed, filling it with some extra protein, to sustain her. It's essential that you continue giving her a proper, nutritious diet at the time that she's nursing.

Last but not the least, if you have no idea what to do once the sow has gone into labor, then seek professional help for it. Let them know in advance so that they will be present. Usually, it's either the inexperience of the sow or the folly of the owner, or both that results in a stillbirth.

Extra Responsibilities
When your mini pig has given birth, you have to ensure the temperature within the pen remains constant. You can regulate it using heat lamps or a fan depending on what the weather outside is. Piglets are usually comfortable between 85-95° F and as they get as old as around six to seven weeks, you can bring the temperature to 70° F.

It would be great if you could arrange for a farrowing pen in addition to the birthing pen so that the sow and newborn piglets can remain disease free. However, a farrowing pen that's been poorly designed will do no good to either of you.

Sanitation is of utmost importance at this time. Hence, you'd also need to remove the manure regularly and to provide some fresh, dry bedding material, especially straw.

Secondly, if the place is too small for them, a piglet can get crushed with the weight of the sow's body if it's not taken out quickly enough. It may also be crushed if the sow, in her attempt to get up, falls over the piglets. It can also be contributed to the fact that their eyesight is not really that great at times and that they are more dependent on their sense of hearing and smell than eyesight. You might want to have on hand goat's milk (fresh is best) and polyvisor baby vitamin with iron, as the pigs are all born iron deficient. Use rubber gloves if you are helping deliver a baby that's stuck. Have some alcohol iodine in a med cup and dip the cords in them quickly at birth to prevent infection.

All the babies can be returned to her for nursing and to get the colostrum they require once she had crossed the afterbirth stage. The babies will fight for the milk. The 'mama' pig will be making low grunting sounds while pushing the milk down so when she quits, you know it's going to be some while, another two hours at least, before the next feeding commences. If, however, the runts are not attempting to fight to nurse, you'd have to be there either for assisting or feeding all of them together with your own hand.

They can be weaned at four weeks of age – that is if you want to give any one of them away – but make sure that it is provided a balanced feed in its growing stages.

Don't forget to notify a teacup pig registrar in your area! The procedure needs to be dealt with in the first forty days of the birth.

Extra Risks
Newborn piglets need special care. There's no limit to how often you need to check to know that both the mother and her babies are healthy.

- The first few days are critical for the young ones particularly as they are at risk of hypothermia. Place a couple of rigid heating pads around them as a source of supplementary heat.
- Their sharp canines can injure the sow, which is nursing them or their siblings during a fight. So yes, they have to be cut off as well.
- They can turn anemic with the rapid growth they usually experience. Ask the vet for the correct dosage of iron injections to prevent it.
- A neonatal would be dependent on the nutrients that's he's getting from milk until about 2 weeks of age. After that, it's safe to introduce them to a starter ration.
- The baby pigs from a miniature tend to shed their skin. As soon as they are one to two weeks old, you might be able to notice the change. The dry, flaky sort of skin that they develop is especially prominent for black pigs. This is a natural process, related usually to stress, lactation, etc, and you don't need to worry about it unless you feel that it's excessive and/or persistent,

for which the vet can recommend a supplement. Otherwise, a good shampooing and moisturizer may restore the glossy coat.

• You might want to consider getting them on the treatment program for an infestation of external parasites (lice, mite). Plus, they won't be able to tell apart unhealthy food from the healthy one or might develop a habit of overeating. Either way, there are high possibilities for them to get diarrhea. Seeing how they are susceptible to these, vaccinations for rhinitis, internal parasites, and pseudo rabies virus should be given early in life too.

Talk to the vet for consultation whether it's best to give initial immunization shots to the piglets or to administer them after the birth.

An orphan piglet
You should consider this a sad occurrence as well. It leaves you as a surrogate mother to your miniature's piglet. You can keep them in a playpen or a pet carrier and apart from using heating pads, you can drape sheets around them to keep them warm. Choose an option that is both convenient to you and comfortable to the piglet for it's going to be dependent on it for at least two weeks after birth. A more pressing concern, however, will be to feed it. You can use an eyedropper to carefully feed it some milk. Goat's milk can be preferred over the commercial sow milk replacer. You'd have to warm it first and feed it after every two hours.

DO NOT give it a pan or a bottle to drink it from; don't opt for the oldest trick in the book either: twisting a towel corner and letting it suck on it may not work. With either possibility, they can drown or choke; a dropper can serve as a safe alternative.

They might struggle as they get older. It is okay if you introduce them to a small flat dish or the bottle by then. Hold the piglet in your lap and use the other hand to introduce it. It will get the idea with time. With the dish, the idea is to get them onto solid foods more easily; with a bottle, you would have to wean them for both the milk and the bottle.

Chapter 4) Things to Consider Before Surrendering a Mini Pig

As much as we would want to believe that we can actually be a good parent for our little baby, the opposite might be the case. While we may have done our homework and provided for its excellent care, circumstances might not let us keep them anymore, caring might become impossible and giving them up for adoption might seem like a good idea. Or you may have gotten one only to decide later that you do not *want* it. Whatever the case, it is, understandably, undesirable and painful for both the pet and the owner.

Pigs are intelligent beings. In the short time that these little creatures might have spent with you, they will become really attached to your family and depressed too at the time of separation. This is why it was stressed in the beginning that you would do better by doing your homework first.

You will need to or find help to get the right family for your pig, to see if they have a piggy compatible home for example and to ensure that your baby does get the care and support you wished for it in the first place.

1) What to Look for in Individuals

a) Does the local zoning approve of mini pigs as pets?
You must hold on until you can find a home that has it in writing. It's <u>important</u>. Say they do meet the other (following) demands, you may suggest that they look for ways they can get the local commissioners to reconsider zoning for the future and to wait until then.
It would be your fault if you placed a pig in an area they are not allowed to be in in the first place. If there's any bright side to it, more and more places are allowing it given the surge in the

popularity of having mini pigs as pets. So, verify it first and get periodic updates from them.

b) Do they have their own home or is it to rent?
This is another factor that you have to consider seeing how the landowner's approval has to be sought first before a mini pig can be kept as a pet. Furthermore, you can also ask them to insure its safety in writing for the contract.

c) Are they familiar with the separate requirements for indoor and outdoor pet pigs?
If the person is an ill prepared owner, it can warn you off from getting your pig being "dumped" anywhere else.
As a rule, they must have a fenced pen or a yard as a place to give your mini pigs some quality time outside. And just like you took the measures with respect to shelter and water availability, "pig proofing" it if there were any pots that you thought would have been ruined with their frequent rooting etc. a prospective adopter should be ready to take these measures too.

d) What about having other pig(s)?
You can ask them whether they have one already or not. You can also test them whether they already know that pigs are herd animals and if they could give some serious thought to adopting another pig along with this one or some time later.
Other Pets: Secondly, check if the new owners have other animals as pets or not. Where pigs generally get along with cats, ferrets and rabbits, they typically do not get along with dogs. So, does the potential adopter understand this and do you, who knows the pig's behavior so well as his current owner, think your pig can adjust with the other animals?

e) Is the person willing to keep it in proper conditions?
That is have they arranged for a local vet as well as the desired mode of transportation as the pig grows up to get it treated for regular observations? They are not many vets who can take care of these teacups. If the owner is ok for these visits, give them time to locate one at least.

As far as transportation is concerned, you might also want them to guarantee that they are aware of the state laws regarding it. This for example can include the need to have them tested by a certified professional before they can take them on a vacation.

f) Are they good parents themselves?
Last but not the least, as a parent taking the decision, you get to decide whether these people are well versed to be pig parents themselves. Because if they are not, chances are it might land you with the pig again or worse, to be dumped elsewhere.

2) What to Look for in a Sanctuary
We all know how fraudulent schemes have been committed by different agencies operating as rescues. Their place and their practices are not so popularly know. Plus, being a good one, they may be overcrowded and already pushed to their limits without being forced to share your burden too.

It is your responsibility to find a good sanctuary for your pig(s). and the following things might let it qualify:

a) They will have a proper education program
They will be clear on their terms regarding the health measures taken. They will be promoting spaying and neutering the pigs before adopting unless health restrictions like severe obesity or old age prevents it. They will not be promoting breeders or allowing breeding in their grounds, encouraging a healthy diet etc. You get the picture.

b) They will be properly facilitated
Most of the good ones are not non-profit but are private. You must take time to ask other rescues and do a little research – not skim – over their work ethics even if you are impressed otherwise.

Remember, if the following are your reasons to leave your mini pigs, then these can be easily corrected:

• Not using the litter box when the need arises

- Tearing up flooring and/or eating through the walls
- Aggressively biting and/or charging at someone
- Breaking into refrigerator and cupboards despite several measures taken to improve it

This is just bad behavior and can be remedied if properly dealt with in time. You can for example make sure that they have not been

- Kept in the house 24/7
- Bored with nothing to do, especially when you are not present
- Enticed to be aggressive

Chapter 5) Euthanasia or "Good Death"

Where saying goodbye to our little beloved pig is already bad enough for us, we are troubled more so when we are the ones to decide that it's time to let it go.

The topic is a sensitive one to tread because of the religious, moral, medical, ethical, financial, and sometimes legal restrictions that are associated with it.

Reasons like divorce or moving to another state can however necessitate that he has to be put down if the already overburdened sanctuaries refuse to take them in. But the main reason it seems is when these pint-size pigs get to be old and suffer or to be bigger than what were originally promised to owners that the latter are to get them euthanized. Although the decision is very much yours to make, it does not entail that you should make the difficult choice on your own.

Owners need to be educated that this unpleasant procedure is only recommended medically if the mini pigs are sick and suffering and have exhausted other solutions and/or have little to zero chance at recovery.

A certified vet would have the required training and means to ease and put the animal out of its misery humanely. However, there may be times when the vet cannot be taken as the first choice for some pet owner. These include (a) that the vet is not available when needed; (b) the owner cannot afford the cost; (c) the transportation may prove to be too disturbing for the pet, making them uncomfortable and fearful when you want their final hours to be soothing.

The list is not exhaustive and as such, there are people who would attempt administering euthanasia at home with varying degrees of success.

The following is the one method that's been approved of by the American Veterinary Medical Association (AVMA). It's considered safe to be used at home.

Carbon dioxide, a component of natural air, is nearly odorless and heavier than air. If administered in low concentrations, i.e. 7.5%, it can serve as a pain reliever; at medium concentrations, i.e. 30-40%, it may be preferred as an anesthetic that would put out the creature without distressing it. A distressed pig would release odors and vocalize; if there are other pigs in the vicinity, it can clearly upset them too. Plus, a large sow or boar would be difficult to control.

Owners should take special care not to overdo it in their first attempt and give a high concentration because it would prove extremely painful, irritating both the respiratory tract and eyes of the tiny pig, and effectively kill the basic tenet of the process.

It is recommended that they be given the analgesic effect first with the lighter dosage, which, within 1-2 minutes approximately, be increased to induce the anesthesia. It is only after this that they are to be given the high concentration. To make it simpler as a standard procedure, the AVMA approves of the use of CO_2 cylinders because the compression would allow for the users to be able to regulate it.

It can also be purchased in a solid state as "dry ice" to establish the depressant and anesthetic effects rapidly. To count off other advantages, it is non-flammable, inexpensive, and has minimal hazards when properly designed equipment is used for it.

On the downside, it can prolong the time for euthanasia if the animal is immature.

That being said, there are other measures too that are capable to (a) cause the brain to slide into a depressive state; (b) decrease the oxygen supply to the brain; and (c) cause physical damage to the brain tissue. These include:

- Captive Bolt Pistol

111

- Stunning
- Gunshot
- Electrocution
- Nitrogen
- Barbituric Acid Derivatives

But again, not all of these are economical, reliable, non-traumatic for the operator and more importantly minimizing animal stress, and producing a rapid loss of consciousness and/or death with pain.

Conclusion

At the end of it all, having a miniature pig is more like having an adopted child. You have to feed it, keep it clean, teach it etiquettes, look out for it, make sure the house is safe before bringing the baby home, and understand what the baby needs.

Babies cannot speak, nor can they express their inner most feelings about what they want. As a parent, it is your duty to look out for them, protect them and take care of them.

Miniature pigs need special attention all the time. You have to make sure they are safe with every change in weather and make sure they have a clean place to stay all the time. This is the difference between the usual farm breed and miniatures, they need special treatment.

Make sure you take them for regular checkups; keep them safe and away from disease causing agents, and harsh weather. Train them with tricks and have fun with them. They can be a joy to have around.

Moreover, here is a reminder once more, before you purchase the pig; make sure the breeder can provide you with a health certificate and proper registration so that transportation would not be a problem for you.

Now that you've read it all, you are set to be a wonderful and proud miniature piggy owner

Published by IMB Publishing 2015

CPSIA information can be obtained
at www.ICGtesting.com
Printed in the USA
LVOW01s1347140116

470653LV00024B/672/P